ABOUT THE BOOK

The *Last Guard Out* is the fascinating true story of one man's life as a guard behind the merciless concrete walls of Alcatraz. I was newly assigned to the infamous island penitentiary of Alcatraz. Reporting to Alcatraz required me to uproot my wife Cathy and young son Kenny from Colorado to California. As we approached San Francisco via the Oakland Bay Bridge we got our first foreboding glance of Alcatraz Island. A strange sense of dread came over me. I looked at our young son asleep on the back seat, then turned to my wife and whispered "What the hell did we do?" After moving to Alcatraz our thoughts on the island quickly changed and we decided not to apply for a transfer out. This left us there until the island closed in March of 1963. Because of our newborn daughter's foot problem we continued living on Alcatraz until June of 1963 making me:

The Last Guard Out

LAST GUARD OUT

A Riveting Account by the Last Guard to Leave Alcatraz

Jim Albright

authorHOUSE®

AuthorHouse™
1663 Liberty Drive
Bloomington, IN 47403
www.authorhouse.com
Phone: 1-800-839-8640

First published by AuthorHouse 4/30/2010

ISBN: 978-1-4343-5077-0 (sc)

Library of Congress Control Number: 2008900759

Printed in the United States of America
Bloomington, Indiana

This book is printed on acid-free paper.

Front cover photo of Alcatraz courtesy of istockphoto. Back cover photo of prison tower, Alcatraz island and cell courtesy of istockphoto.

INTRODUCTION

This book, "The Last Guard Out", is about a young man from Iowa with a wife and young son, with no prior law enforcement experience or training who ended up a guard at Alcatraz. As time goes by, fewer and fewer people who worked there or were incarcerated there will be alive to debate, discuss and record the stories and experiences that are associated with "The Rock". To the best of my knowledge, and after visiting the island during recent reunions, the feeling is that the number is now probably less than 100. I felt we are at that point where the years keep robbing us of eye-witnesses. I had a sense of urgency to finish this book and although I am not a good writer, I wanted to try to capture my personal experiences and share that knowledge, so that it could be passed on to others. I decided not to go into a lot of history, as that can be found in many other books. Also, I wanted to focus on my family's involvement and what occurred while I was there. I rank Alcatraz with such historical significances as "Devil's Island" and "The Alamo."

"The Last Guard Out" is intended to not only bring light to some of the truths about the history of Alcatraz, but to dispel some of the myths such as the one about Alcatraz personnel catching sharks and cutting off one fin so they would swim in circles around the island to deter escapes. And to point out the difficulties that the guards had dealing with inmates.

In spite of many obstacles and with the encouragement from friends and relatives, I'm glad I wrote this book for myself and my family. Here, preserved forever in one place, are all those memories from a very special time in our lives.

I had lots of help and suggestions on what to put into this book. To those individuals I'm forever grateful. Their support meant so much to me; especially John and Marilyn Peters. Finally, a special thanks to my family – Cathy, Kenny, Vicki and Donna.

CHAPTER ONE

"Final call for Alcatraz! All aboard!," shouted the Blue and Gold Fleet deck hand as the captain throttled the ship's diesel engines. Nearby, a group of seals flopped on floating docks and began to noisily bark their protests as the people they had just entertained were being ferried away from Pier 41 and out into San Francisco Bay.

Twenty-eight years had passed since I locked the doors to the cellhouse and left behind "The Rock" with my wife Cathy and three young children Kenny, Vicki, and Donna to begin a new life in Marion, Illinois. I wondered if the original key to the cellhouse, which I have, would still work. The key was at my home in Indiana and I wouldn't have the opportunity to find out. Several opportunities to return to the island had availed themselves since that day in 1963 but, for one reason or another, our return would be postponed. Invitation letters to the island's annual resident reunion were mailed yearly to our house in Indiana, but it wasn't until August 14, 1991, that Cathy, my sister "Beanie" (Marilyn), brother- in-law John, and

1

I decided to make the cross-country trip back to San Francisco. This date also coincided with the 32nd anniversary of my start date as a 24-year-old rookie Alcatraz guard.

I stared intently over the ship's bow as we sped across the bay on the mile and a quarter trip to Alcatraz. The first boat I had taken on this journey, the 1930s era Warden Johnston, wasn't nearly as swift and was roughly a quarter the size of this modern vessel. This ship made a mockery of the small waves hitting its hull, in sharp contrast to the sometimes rough, bronco-like rides of the smaller Warden Johnston.

The bay was calm and the sun shone brightly on the light brown island cliffs and green vegetation crawling towards the sea. The familiar sites of Angel Island, Treasure Island, the Oakland Bay Bridge and the Golden Gate Bridge surrounded us like old friends. The sounds of seagulls filled the air and a flock of pelicans also passed by. Several sailboats could be seen dotting the waters and a couple of playful seals were seen breaching and then disappearing back down into the watery darkness.

There had been many times on this crossing when the fog and mist were so thick that you could barely see your hand in front of your face. Although this day was clear, a mist slowly began to cover my eyes.

Returning to the island was something I had dreamed about for many years. During our many moves throughout my 26 year career with the Federal Bureau of Prisons, we had always looked back upon our 4 years at Alcatraz with fondness. Although this was viewed by the public as a notorious place which held "the worst of the worst", living on the island was a unique and enjoyable experience. In fact, I have often told people that I could have easily spent my entire career on Alcatraz if it had remained in operation.

Many happy memories came flooding back to me as we drew within a couple hundred yards of the shore. Taking Kenny to the mainland for his first day of kindergarten, island kids playing on the parade ground, residents helping each other bring groceries onto the boat, Cathy and the kids waiting for me on the apartment balcony as I finished my shift on boat patrol -- those were just some of things that made this cold, bare rock a warm place to live.

These memories were soon tempered, however, by sights of the dramatic changes that had taken place on the island over the past 30 years. Buildings which once stood prominently at the edge of the old army parade ground facing San Francisco were completely gone and replaced by piles of twisted metal and concrete. The trademark lighthouse was still intact and functioning, but the formerly attached and architecturally splendid lighthouse keeper's home was gone. The once beautiful warden's residence stood as a ghostly shell outlined against the pale blue sky. It looked like a bomb had gone off on the south end of the island. Perhaps fittingly, the only south end structure still intact was the cranky, old fog signal building near the shoreline, which, along with its sister building on the north end, had driven many residents nuts on foggy days.

As much as I looked forward to this visit, the destruction of the island over the past 30 years would be difficult to swallow. I would try to keep an open mind and focus on the positive memories, but the destruction that stood before us was a painful reminder of the neglect and abuse the island had suffered following its closure.

Rounding the southeast corner of the island a familiar sign became visible: "Warning: Persons Procuring or Concealing Escape of Prisoners are Subject to Prosecution." This sign had been used to help keep boaters outside the 300 yard limit from Alcatraz's shore line.

As we prepared to dock, I looked up and saw our old apartment building. Still visible on the sides of the building were large letters "Indians Welcome." This was painted during the 1969-1971 period when Native Americans briefly occupied the island after laying territorial claim. This was also a period of great destruction to island buildings. Several buildings were burned during this period and the interiors of surviving buildings were gutted for firewood and other materials. Graffiti was etched and sprayed throughout the island as an intended permanent reminder of the Native American cause.

Of particular note was Memorial Day weekend, 1970, when the Native Americans invited all San Franciscans to come to the island for a weekend celebration of Native American culture. Thousands flocked onto the island and the end result was serious destruction and fires being set to existing structures. To this day, it is uncertain whether it was the Native Americans, overzealous visitors or government provocateurs who set the fires. The eventual losers from this destruction were the Native Americans themselves and future generations of island visitors who will never get to see it in its former glory.

Our docking was smooth and a modern hydraulic ramp greeted the edge of the boat. Again, this was in sharp contrast to the old boat ramp 30 yards to the north which consisted of an angle iron covered by wood which was raised and lowered by a winch in conjunction with the tides. The Fort Mason mainland docking site was even trickier and essentially consisted of a free-floating platform and ladder which required a gymnast's agility when entering and leaving the boat.

I was in my own world as we stepped off the boat and walked up the aluminum gangway toward the landing area. My mind raced as my eyes soaked up everything around me like a sponge. It felt like I was stepping back in time.

My thoughts were soon interrupted when I heard a voice over a bullhorn saying to the crowd, "Ladies and Gentleman, we have a former Alcatraz prison guard, Mr. Jim Albright, with us here today." Unbeknownst to me, my brother-in-law John had slipped through the crowd and tipped off our arrival to the National Park Ranger, John Cantwell. Although I was already somewhat conspicuous with my Federal Bureau of Prisons hat and jacket, there would be no anonymity now. Hundreds of eyes turned toward me as I smiled and made my way toward the podium. Friendly stares were always a welcome sight compared to the many cold, evil stares I'd received during my 26 years in the prison system.

After listening to John Cantwell give a brief history of Alcatraz and an overview of the day's events, he pulled us aside and asked if we would be interested in taking a personal tour of the island. With little hesitation we agreed. After waiting 28 years to return, we certainly wouldn't mind the added personal attention.

John directed us to meet him just outside the Island bookstore after watching a short 10-minute film on the history of Alcatraz in the old cannon battery under the apartments. The cannon battery was part of the original fortress built on Alcatraz in 1852 and a barracks building was added above the structure in 1909 to house U.S. Army prison personnel. In 1934 the barracks were converted into apartments for U.S. Federal prison personnel and their families when Alcatraz switched from a military prison to a maximum security federal penitentiary.

Watching the old film clips reminded me of the former glory of the island and historical role Alcatraz played in the developing western frontier. Few people know that Alcatraz was the largest U.S. military installation west of the Mississippi throughout the mid- to late-1800s. The installation was originally established to protect California gold interests during the rush of the mid-1800s and played a significant role in protecting the San Francisco Bay area from Confederate sympathizers during the U.S. Civil War a decade later. Changing weaponry and stronger cannons rendered the brick-walled fortress on Alcatraz obsolete by 1870 and the island's new roots as a military prison began to take hold.

After briefly browsing the nearby book store, John Cantwell met us and started our tour by taking us into the area behind the apartments known as "Chinatown". This area was given its name for its similarity to the dark, narrow alleyways in San Francisco's famous Chinatown. The brickwork and arched doorways from the 150-year-old military installation added a unique element to Alcatraz's Chinatown.

The initial stop on this guided tour would be our first apartment in what was formerly known as Building 64 which we moved into in November, 1959. We walked to the south end of Chinatown, up a flight of stairs and over to a decaying door marked 108. This was a one-bedroom apartment normally reserved for couples without children or single officers. We had the added challenge of trying to fit into these cramped quarters with an active two-year-old boy. (A year later we'd had enough and moved to a two-bedroom apartment on the third (top) floor at the opposite side of the building).

John Cantwell unlocked the door and, upon entering the apartment, we immediately noticed that the old appliances and cupboards were still intact in the dust-covered, cob-web filled kitchen. "I thought you cleaned this place before we left," I mockingly said to Cathy. The dirty look I received made the filth in the apartment pale by comparison. Nearby, a built-in wall ironing board was deployed and seemingly ready for the next pair of pants to be pressed. As we began walking around, we encountered dirt and debris everywhere. The bathroom was in disrepair and the bathtub and toilet were filled with old plaster and assorted trash. The rusted medicine cabinet was still hanging on for dear life from the crumbling walls. Paint and plaster were peeling from the walls in the dining area (Kenny's former bedroom) and living room. At the front of the living room there was a door which led out onto a shared balcony which ran the length of the building. Even though this was only the first floor, the balcony was still approximately 25 feet above ground-level and afforded occupants with a commanding view of the dock area, guard tower and surrounding East Bay. This would be prime real estate in today's booming Bay area market!

"Seen enough?" John asked us back inside the apartment. We agreed and took our final pictures and glimpses of the sad state of affairs. As a parting shot, Beanie took our picture standing in the doorway with the number 108 prominently displayed between us. This remains one of my favorite pictures from the trip.

As we worked our way across the first floor we passed the old post office which, in relative terms, appeared to be in pretty good shape. The 1930s era light fixture in the main room was still intact and the small shelf and postal window were also preserved. Our visit to the small grocery store next door wasn't as uplifting. The remaining shelves, which hadn't been used for firewood during the Native American occupation, were mainly broken and in disrepair. Two old coolers which once contained meat and other perishables were reduced to rusting hulks adorned with broken glass. The old sinks still remained in the back, but one of them was badly broken. George and Patti Deathridge, who managed the grocery store, would not be happy about this. George was a guard who assisted Patti during his free hours.

Next stop would be our third-story, two-bedroom apartment, number 302. Normally we would access this apartment from a walkway at the back of the building which led straight to the third floor, but Ranger John decided to take us on a shortcut through the first floor apartment of George and Patty Deathridge. While walking through the decrepit remains I noticed a large piece of jagged glass hanging precariously off the edge of the kitchen counter. I leaned over to Cathy and, pointing to the loose shard, said, "Now I know how they got the name 'Deathridge'...". She groaned and rolled her eyes as she had a million times before with my ill humor.

We soon entered a main hallway at the back of the apartment and approached a stairway leading to the second floor. "Stay clear of the railing, it's about ready to fall off," John warned us. These stairs and their surroundings reminded me of a scene in a sci-fi horror film. Broken railings, cobwebs, plaster and paint peeling in large chunks, light fixtures dangling, glass strewn on the floor and the sounds of sea gulls and pigeons echoing throughout the building. To top it off, the stairs leading to the third floor ended mysteriously into the ceiling – the supposed result of an architect's mistake. In actuality, Building 64 was built as an Army barracks. When this building was converted to apartments, the stairway became superfluous and rather than remove it they let it ascend to nowhere. My guess is that the ghosts of Alcatraz still use these stairs today when ascending to the 3rd floor.

Finally, we entered our second island apartment. The scene was now familiar with debris and dust covering the floor and dirt obstructing the view from the tall, narrow windows. The light fixtures were mainly missing, except the one in the kitchen, and the old oven was still intact seemingly ready for Cathy to whip up a batch of her famous cookies. The bathroom was in better shape than the first apartment, but that wasn't saying much. Entering the master bedroom, we noticed that Cathy's makeshift bed sheet curtains were still hanging, stained and tattered, while stapled to boards at the top of the two tall windows. We pulled aside the old fabric and peeked out towards the power plant and the road leading up to the cellhouse. This apartment formed the northwest corner of Building 64 and afforded some unique views that tenants in the middle of the building couldn't match.

After our tour of 302 was complete, we moved across Chinatown, down some stairs and onto the old military Parade Ground. The military laid the concrete for the Parade Ground, and used it mainly for military drills and parade formations. When Alcatraz changed hands from the military to the Federal Government in 1934, the Parade Ground became a play ground and gathering place for families living on the island. In addition, there were new apartments built, gardens grown, and facilities for handball and weightlifting. All this was gone now and replaced by piles of twisted metal and concrete thanks to a Government Services Administration (GSA) decision in the early 1970s to demolish the remaining structures.

With nothing to see on the Parade Ground, we moved back toward the north end of the island and passed the Military Guardhouse, Military Chapel, Electric Repair Shop and Officer's Club. The Guardhouse, Chapel and Repair Shop were in great shape and appeared to have been recently covered with a fresh coat of paint. The Officer's Club, however, was reduced to a concrete shell with metal and wood debris lying upon its foundation -- another casualty of the 1970 Memorial Day weekend fires.

As we continued walking behind the old water tower and prison recreation yard, a westerly breeze delivered an interesting combined scent of seagull guano and saltwater. The Western Gulls had just concluded their nesting season a few weeks earlier and left behind a fresh white coating on the areas they frequented – especially on the Parade Ground and north side where we were currently walking. In the early days, before the military altered the face of the island and barged in soil for lawns and gardens, Alcatraz was mainly comprised of the slippery combination of sandstone and guano. Footing must've been extremely treacherous for the early explorers!

While walking between the New Industries Building and the Model Industries Building, we were greeted by the clanging of a small buoy near Little Alcatraz, a small rock outcropping about 30 yards off the northwestern shore. To the west was the beautiful view of the Golden Gate and Fort Point, another Civil War military installation which fortified the bay in conjunction with the fortress on Alcatraz. Fort Point also has an interesting military history stretching from its Civil War roots to World War I when it was re-commissioned as a military barracks. During World War II a submarine net was stretched from the edge of Fort Point, under the Golden Gate Bridge, and connected to the headlands a mile to the north in an effort to thwart any bold Japanese subs.

The chain link, barbed-wire fencing which followed the perimeter pathway along the western shore was badly rusted and, in many cases, missing or leaning over the edge of the 20 foot cliffs leading down to the bay. John Cantwell warned us that in certain areas of the island we would need to exercise extreme caution -- this was particularly true along this stretch. One wrong step and you'd be crashing down onto the jagged, debris-covered rocks below.

Remnants of the once beautiful gardens still existed along the western side of the cellhouse. During the prison years, a full-time gardener kept these gardens trimmed and vibrant. Although the gardens had now become wild, they still possessed great beauty with flowering plants like roses, nasturtiums, red torch plants, magenta pelargoniums and Japanese honeysuckle. Crepe Myrtle still winds its way down the hills and several trees such as walnut, apple and fig still bear fruit. The larger Pride of Madeira plants have spread from a single plant brought to the island in the 1930s and naturalized along the western side. Artichoke plants, also from the 1930s, still grow on the lower terraces leading down to the bay.

Our walk around the perimeter reminded me of the many days and nights when I was on shore patrol and walked these same paths. I always enjoyed shore patrol because it allowed me the freedom to move around, see the beauty of the island and break the monotony associated with being on watch.

The silence was deafening as we entered the New Industries Building which, during inmate working hours, was always a hub of activity. At any given time the air would be filled with the assorted sounds of clothes washers and dryers, band saws, grinders, hammers and sewing machines operating in the various parts of the building. Shoes and small machinery were repaired, clothes were cleaned, and items such as brooms, brushes, gloves and inmate clothing were produced. The combined scents of laundry detergent, cleaning fluids and other chemicals once filled the air.

I closed my eyes for a moment and envisioned 45 inmates hunched over sewing machines intently eyeing fabric as they produced work gloves by the dozens. The glove shop supervisor walked warily up and down the aisles keeping a watchful eye on his unpredictable workers. I then opened my eyes to the blankness of this cavernous space, broken only by the unique columns which held up the second floor. Cathy and Beanie's voices echoed off the walls as they talked and the wind whistled through the broken panes of glass.

While walking the northern shore, a loud blast from a ship's horn reminded us to look away from the island and back towards the bay. A large Korean container ship was making its way along the north shore heading towards the Golden Gate and eventually out to the Pacific for its long journey home. A Black-Crowned Night Heron squawked nearby while perched upon the north fog signal building.

The silence caught my attention again as we strode the path behind the old Power Plant. The rumble of diesel engines once permeated the area surrounding the plant as direct current electricity was being generated on-site. Black smoke once billowed from the single smokestack and, on days when a strong northerly wind blew, curled itself around the upper levels of the island like a black python. Today, the island's reduced electrical needs are handled by cables delivering alternating current from the mainland. The smokestack has remained clean for many years.

As we ascended the steep hill leading to the cellhouse I was reminded that nearly 30 years had passed since my more youthful body had regularly made this journey. Even though Cathy and I walk nearly every day back in Terre Haute, there aren't many areas in town which compare to the 64 foot climb starting from the dock to the base of the cellhouse. Alcatraz is only 12.5 acres in size, but it's the hills that will wear you down!

We entered the cellhouse at the basement level and went straight to the former clothing room and shower room. The clothing cage still contained some of the old shelving used for towels, bed linens and inmate clothing. Numbers could still be seen under the respected cubbyholes signifying inmates and clothing sizes. When I glanced at the boxes, it brought back memories and I could recall several inmate's names, numbers, clothing sizes, living quarters and job assignments. For example, Alvin Francis Karpovick (AZ 325) better known as ALVIN "CREEPY" Karpis – a member of Ma Barker's gang – resided in an outside cell of C-Block, worked in the Industries, and was of average size. I had spent many days in the cage dispersing clothing and linens to freshly showered inmates.

After walking around the shower room we headed across the hall to the band room. Coincidentally, we met up with one of the oldest surviving Alcatraz officers today, Officer Phil Bergen, who was Captain of the Guards from 1949 to 1955. Captain Bergen actually served on Alcatraz from September, 1939, to July, 1955, and had a reputation for toughness. He had seen some of the most tumultuous times in prison history, including the infamous 1946 break-out attempt where 9 guards were taken hostage and 2 were eventually killed.

After exchanging pleasantries with Captain Bergen we made our way upstairs to the main floor of the cellhouse. The upper landing took place in the former barber shop which sat at the north end of "A" block. The cellhouse consisted of four blocks, A through D, with A being the oldest and least used.

Traveling through A Block was always interesting because graffiti from the early military prisoners was still evident on the cell walls. These walls remained unpainted for many years and, ironically, this kept a piece of Alcatraz history alive. The Native Americans later added their commentary in interesting contrast to the early 20th century military graffiti.

John Cantwell shined his flashlight down a dark stairway located at the mid-point of A Block. This was an entry point for the notorious "dungeons" of Alcatraz. In military days, unruly prisoners were supposedly sent to this dank, musty place to endure endless torture and hardship for their improprieties. Prisoners were supposedly chained to the walls, stripped of their clothing, beaten senseless and left to endure rats, raw sewage, cockroaches and the dark, bone-chilling dampness. The dungeons were never used by the Federal Bureau of Prisons, although early federal penitentiary prisoners may beg to differ. As a matter of fact, it did not exist as such while I was there. Where the old dungeon once stood was nothing but a big hole. I personally inspected it out of curiosity.

At the south end of A Block we turned right and headed two blocks west before traveling up the main walkway between Blocks B and C known as "Broadway." I soaked up the view of the cellhouse and was surprised to see how well preserved it was. The main floor cells, known as "The Flats", had obviously been re-painted and many of the cell commodes, sinks and flip-down tables and seats were still intact. The floor wasn't spit-polished clean like it had been during prison years, but years of wax still afforded it with a dull luster. Paint was peeling from the 4-story high ceiling, but the window skylights appeared to be unbroken and intact. On the north end of Broadway, a single, large wall clock still kept accurate time in an area known as "Times Square."

Midway down Broadway, we turned through a service access corridor to the walkway between A and B Blocks known as "Michigan Avenue". We read wall plaques containing information on some of the more famous prisoners like Al Capone, George "Machine Gun" Kelly, Doc Barker, Robert "The Birdman" Stroud, Alvin "Creepy" Karpis and L.A. mobster Mickey Cohen.

We entered the former dining area and I was struck by how empty it looked without dining tables, chairs, steam tables, etc. The brown linoleum floor was peeling in several spots revealing an early 20th century black and white tile floor which I had previously only seen in the kitchen area. Several tear gas canisters were still affixed to the support columns and outside walls. Behind a set of bars, the kitchen looked well-preserved and ready to serve the next meal. A menu board still displayed the final meal choices before the prison's closure on March 21, 1963. A kitchen tools cabinet showing the outline of various knives and other sharp utensils was prominently displayed for public viewing. These were known as "Shadow Boards" as all knives, etc. were painted on the board so the guard could easily identify if a utensil was missing. These boards were kept under lock and key except when issued by an officer.

Upon leaving the dining area, John walked us over to a stairway which led to the second floor hospital. This is where the strip cells, operating rooms, X-ray facilities, pharmacy, doctor's offices and the isolated cell of The Birdman were located. Initially, the Park Service allowed the public to tour the hospital, but personnel cutbacks made the premises too risky to be left unattended, and was put off limits to tourists. Underneath the stairway to the right was the mug shot room where vital statistics and photographs of new arrivals were recorded. Annual pictures of all prisoners were also taken at this location.

We traveled up the lonely staircase to the second floor and John Cantwell revealed an original, oversized prison key which he used to open the locked gate leading to the hospital. It was eerily dark and quiet in the hospital hallway and dust-filled rays of light shined through the open doorways of westerly-facing rooms. Our first stop was in a nearby strip cell whose floors were incredibly clean and yellow tiles sparkled in the afternoon light. Next door, the old pharmacy was still in good shape and, although the drug counter top was missing, the counter base and tall cabinets behind it were well-preserved. The nearby operating room still had a large overhead light fixture. This light had been used during surgery, but now was broken. A therapeutic bathtub sat quietly in the corner of the therapy room and, upon closer inspection, contained a dead, brown mouse lying in the debris. The x-ray room still contained equipment and we opened a cabinet with narrow file drawers to find remnants of unused x-ray film. Our final hospital stop was Robert Stroud's large cell which was entirely vacant except for a single easel holding a story board describing his fascinating, yet strange, life behind bars.

After departing the hospital and re-entering the main cellhouse, I was intrigued to see a well-preserved wooden Bull Durham tobacco dispenser affixed to the wall across from the National Park Service information desk. Inmates were allowed to access the dispenser following meals and when going to and from the recreation yard. The smell of Bull Durham hand-rolled cigarette smoke wafted throughout the cellhouse daily and was one of the few privileges afforded to inmates.

We departed the cellhouse and took the outside stairs leading down to the recreation yard on the western end of the dining hall. The tiered steps where inmates once sat to play chess, checkers, dominoes and other approved games were now crumbling and dangerous. The catwalk which followed the western edge of the dining hall was gone, but its base was still evident by short strips of jagged metal protruding every 5 feet from holes in the side of the building. Painted outlines of shuffleboard triangles were still evident on the recreation yard floor as were the painted lines where prisoners gathered to be counted before heading to their various industry jobs. A rusting baseball backstop sat lonely in the northwest corner while the old water tower and yard guard tower loomed over the northeast corner.

We went back inside and turned right into D Block, which was also known as "segregation" or "the hole".

We concluded our cellhouse tour by walking through the library, up the north end of C Block to the location of the 1946 cellhouse shootings and then back down to the south end near the prisoner visitation area. "Where to next?" Ranger John asked. Like a kid in a candy store, I immediately pointed to a large "lock box" on the wall at the south end of C block. "Mind if I tried my hand at opening and closing the cell doors?" I asked. "Not at all," John replied, "Let's go to the second tier to get away from the crowds".

Excitedly, I followed John up the stairway to the second tier where an identical lock box was located. Cathy, Beanie and brother-in-law John must have thought I was going crazy, but they followed along behind us. I opened the lock box door exposing a set of levers and mechanisms which required some training to operate. Would I remember how to do this after 35 years? Slowly I selected the door numbers, pulled down the lever and then brought the lever back to its upright position. The sound of doors sliding along tracks as they opened followed my upward arm movement. Again, I pulled the lever down and then brought it back up. The sweet sound of steel meeting steel reverberated throughout the concrete building as the doors slammed shut. For good measure, I practiced a few more times to make sure I remembered how to operate the system and a crowd gathered below to watch the demonstration. I can't explain it, but the sound of those doors closing sent chills up my spine and gave me great satisfaction. Apparently I'm not alone, because George Lucas recorded the same sounds for the closing of space ship doors in his Star Wars films. Movie personnel visited Alcatraz after it closed and, when the doors were opened and shut, they were impressed with the sound and used it in the movie. I remember seeing the movie and when I heard the sound it brought back memories.

Our day was beginning to get short as John took us to the east end where the chapel, officer's mess, and east gun gallery were located. The chapel, which also doubled as a movie room, still contained the altar and a large set of risers with neat rows of folding chairs from top to bottom. Next door, the wood paneling in the officer's mess had been removed and used as firewood during the Native American occupation exposing two by fours and wiring. We squeezed up the narrow stairway into the east gun gallery for a final view of the main cellhouse before heading to the roof, where we viewed the vent and escape route taken by the Anglin Brothers and Morris during the escape of 1962. We had a spectacular view of the entire island and the Bay area. This brought tears to my eyes and brought back many memories.

We proceeded down the stairs towards the front gate. We stopped to peek in the glass windows where the prison control room once operated. I had operated many of these knobs and buttons during my shifts as a control room officer while communicating with various locations on the island and throughout the world on the telephone switchboard. The original microphone and telephone still sat on the counter and so did a Rolodex containing yellowed index cards with key outside phone numbers.

We stepped out of the main cellhouse door to be greeted by the westerly breezes and spectacular view of the San Francisco skyline. Ironically, this great view was made possible by the fact that the lighthouse keeper's residence had burned down 24 years ago. The trademark white lighthouse, built in 1909, and fully automated after the prison closed in 1963, rose 84 feet directly above us. The night before, while strolling along Fisherman's Wharf, we were warmed to see its' beacon shining brightly in the bay.

We peered into the remaining shell of the warden's residence. The rubble of this magnificent home was one of the most sickening sights on the island. All that was left inside was the remnants of a first floor marble fireplace and rotted timbers The gardens on the south side of the house were in ruins, but several flowers still grew unattended including dark red tea roses, yellow roses and Firecracker Fuschia. I still preferred the order and weed-free beauty of the tended gardens myself.

We slowly wound our way back down the cobblestone paths leading to the dock area to catch the 4:30 PM boat. This was a lot easier on the body than the trip up! After crossing through the old salleyport and landing on the flats of the dock area we thanked John Cantwell for generously providing us with a day-long, VIP tour. It had been a full, exciting day packed with nostalgia and memories. Seven hours had passed in the blink of an eye as we departed feeling energized and openly wondering why we had taken so long to return.

As we pulled away from the dock, I stood at the rear of the boat watching the island slowly fade into the distance. Returning to Alcatraz had impacted me in ways I could not have imagined. It felt like I had just spent the day getting re-acquainted with an aging, old friend. The years had not been kind to her, but the underlying beauty was still there.

CHAPTER TWO

The nicknames of many of the characters who lived on Alcatraz were generally colorful, descriptive, and hyped by the media to stir the imagination of the American public. People such as "Machine Gun" Kelley, Alvin "Creepy" Karpis, Al "Scarface" Capone, and Robert "The Birdman" Stroud were being watched by "goon squad" guards and lieutenants named "Double Tough". With this aura of toughness and fear etched into American mindset, how did the kid nicknamed "Wimpy" from a small Midwestern town become an Alcatraz guard?

My journey to Alcatraz began in Washington, Iowa, on April 8, 1935, where I was the fifth out of seven children born to Bill and Alice Albright. My father worked as a journeyman electrician while my mom had her hands full staying at home raising two boys and five girls. By social standards we were upper-lower class and a typical Midwestern family.

Living in a small town had its benefits, but high-paying jobs were not one of them. By 1937 my parents had grown tired of stretching to feed seven hungry kids, so we moved to Iowa City where jobs were more plentiful and wages were higher. My father's talents were recognized early by a small Iowa City family business, Mulford Electric, and he was hired on the spot.

We settled into a 5-bedroom house on the south side of Iowa City which was located near the Rock Island Train Depot and directly across the street from a railhead for loading and unloading cars. Having the depot and railhead nearby was an ideal situation for a small boy who loved trains and shiny, new automobiles from Detroit. My buddies and I would often spend time watching the rail hands and helping them with their tasks. If we were lucky, the rail hands would "accidentally" bust a box of candy from a railcar and reward us with a pocketful for our efforts.

When candy supplies got low, the kids always migrated up the street to Tony Ronella's grocery store where penny candy, sodas and bad jokes were the menu of the day. We'd then burn our sugar off by playing games like kick the can, "mother may I", tag, football, baseball, and basketball; often till past dark when you couldn't see the hoop.

As a child, I could best be described as a stubborn, yet fun-loving, agitator (note: my family and friends may argue that I've carried these traits forward into adulthood). I could always be counted on to provide smart aleck remarks and play practical jokes upon my friends and siblings. In fact, I was responsible for many of my sisters' childhood nicknames. With turnabout being fair play, I was nicknamed "Wimpy" for my love of hamburgers and "Ferdinand the Bull" due to my bull-headed, stubborn disposition.

Our entire family had a strong, Midwestern work ethic and the Albright kids all did their fair share of jobs to help the family cause. At an early age, I began spending time with my dad as he made his rounds doing electrical jobs. I was always on standby to provide tools or act as a "gopher" when items were missing from his tool chest. My dad worked long hours and working at his side afforded me the rare chance to spend valuable time with him. He even worked at home repairing people's pocket watches and was compensated not only monetarily, but also with food items such as beef, poultry and vegetables.

I was 10 when I started my first real job delivering both the Cedar Rapids Gazette morning paper and the Iowa City Press-Citizen after school. At 12, I moved on to working in a duck-pin bowling alley setting pins and, a year later when the alley upgraded into full-scale bowling lanes, I worked dropping pins into the semi-automated racks.

Following my bowling alley experience, I hired on with a local lawn mowing firm which, heaven help the people of Iowa City, taught me how to drive a vehicle. By the time I was 15, however, it was time to leave the dirt and grime of the lawn mowing business and work in a local roller skating rink. Not only was the roller rink cleaner, but it provided one key benefit for a young man that my other jobs couldn't match – GIRLS!!

In my first few weeks at the roller rink, I began noticing a particularly attractive 14-year-old brunette girl whom I had also seen in the halls at school. She was a pretty good skater, but I was especially struck by her beautiful blue eyes. Never being one to shy away from a situation, I quickly got up the nerve to introduce myself and soon found out she appeared to be as interested in me as I was her. Her name was Cathy and the rest, as they say, is history.

Cathy and I soon began spending a lot more time together both during and after school. She lived on a farm on the far south side of Iowa City and had an after-school job working in a local movie theatre. It was an ideal situation for a young couple– free roller rink passes and free movie passes.

My fun-loving, agitating style never turned Cathy away, but did provide for some interesting moments in our relationship. One time I took her shoes off at school and threw them into an empty locker. Shoeless, she walked down to the principal's office to report the incident and ended up getting into further trouble for letting me take her shoes in the first place. Needless to say, a few days passed before she let me hold her hand in the school hallway again.

Cathy and I had dated for one year when my parents decided to move the family to Denver, CO, for new job opportunities. I was now in the 10th grade, had a steady girlfriend and wasn't interested in moving. I informed my parents before their departure that I was going to stay back in Iowa City and live with my buddy Don Mahanna and his mother Nell. Reluctantly, my parents agreed.

Shortly after my family moved to Denver, I ended up dropping out of high school and began working as a full-time mechanic in a local car dealership, Nall Motors. I maintained part-time hours at the roller rink so Cathy and I could still enjoy free skating. She, on the other hand, left the movie theatre for a higher paying job at the University of Iowa Hawkeye bookstore. Getting discounts on books wasn't nearly as exciting as free movie passes, however.

Life in the years immediately following my family's departure had its ups and downs. The first summer after they left, I actually traveled back to Denver for 3 months with a buddy, Steve Maxey, to live with my parents and work in a paper box factory. I quickly returned to Iowa City, however, to be with Cathy. Her family had just moved into the city from the farm and this made things more convenient.

Cathy continued through high school and we spent as much time as possible going on dates and watching school events such as football and basketball games. I raised a little hell on the side by pulling pranks such as tying a bicycle inner tube to a car exhaust and driving down the street while the car made a loud "BBBRRRAAAPPP" sound. The Iowa City police didn't find this too funny, however, and I had to call Cathy to come pick me up at the local precinct.

By the time I was 19, Cathy had graduated and I fully realized the pivotal role she played in my life. She had been a stabilizing factor during a time of personal upheaval and provided much-needed love and companionship. I wasn't destined for a life of crime but, without her influence, I might not have stayed on the right path. Realizing Cathy's importance to me, I bought a ring and, on her 18th birthday, asked for her hand in marriage at the roller rink. She happily agreed and I was the luckiest guy alive.

On April 30th, 1955, we were married and 6-months later bought our first house in Iowa City. We maintained our jobs at Nall Motors and the Hawkeye Bookstore, but had the itch to move on to bigger and better things. By 1957, Cathy was pregnant and we decided it was time to make the break from Iowa. Much to the surprise of friends and family, we announced we were packing up and moving to Denver, CO.

In June, 1957, we bought a two-bedroom house in the suburb of Aurora just outside of Denver. Shortly after we settled in, our only son, Kenny, was born and life changed significantly for the two of us. Cathy stayed at home to care for our newborn and I took the first job available which involved loading trucks at the local Sealtest Dairy.

Working at Sealtest proved to be a back-breaking job. I was one of a couple young, strong men working in the cooler loading large milk containers onto trucks. During a 5-hour period, it was not uncommon to personally lift several tons of milk onto waiting trucks. This type of weight lifting certainly built upper body strength, but would tear any man apart after a few years.

By late 1958, Cathy was expecting again and we anxiously awaited the arrival of our second child. A sweet girl, Linda Sue, was born on January 25, 1959, but died from complications 5-days later. The loss of Linda was devastating to both of us.

1959 turned out to be one heck of a bad year. We were recovering from the loss of Linda when my grandmother died in the spring. Two months after returning from grandma's funeral in Iowa City, my mother suddenly passed away. This fully supported the theory that bad things happened in "threes".

The loss of our family members jolted us into re-focusing on our own future. Loading milk trucks wasn't going to ensure my long-term health and my benefits package was sub-par at best. I began actively looking for a better paying job which offered good medical benefits and a retirement package. My brother-in-law, Al Leiseth, worked in nearby Englewood, CO, at the federal prison and encouraged me to look into a job there. The government paid well and the benefits package was certainly attractive. I obtained an application and sent it in to the prison personnel office.

Not long after submitting my federal application, I was invited into Englewood for an interview, aptitude test, and medical exam.

This wasn't a guarantee that I'd make it into the prison system, but it was certainly a step in the right direction.

I waited a few weeks after taking my exams when the Englewood warden informed me that there was a hiring freeze at the prison and little likelihood I'd be hired in the near future. It was rumored that federal jobs would soon be offered at a new federal prison in Minnesota, but nothing was forthcoming from the government.

Finally, after waiting a few more weeks, a letter arrived from the U.S. Government in Washington, D.C. Cathy handed me the envelope and I hastily opened it to see if a job offer was inside and where it might be located. My heart raced as I saw the word "congratulations" appear in the first sentence. My heart soon sank, however, as I saw the location of the appointment: "U.S.P. Alcatraz".

Never in my wildest dreams did I think I would be asked to start as a rookie guard with no prior training or experience in any form of law enforcement and to be assigned to the most notorious and toughest prison in the United States. After all, Alcatraz was meant for seasoned guards that were "tough as nails" and used to handling the "worst of the worst". I was physically fit from the daily grind of lifting milk containers, but was I prepared to handle the nasty men locked up on The Rock?

Cathy was in shock and disbelief after seeing the appointment location. 1959 had already been a crazy year for us, and now our "big opportunity" was a one-way ticket to Alcatraz?? What in the world did we do to deserve all this??

We spent a couple weeks mulling over the job offer and finally came to the conclusion that we'd accept the position, spend one year of government "probation" time on Alcatraz, and then immediately transfer back to Englewood. Short-term it would be a hassle, but we had to think about long-term job security and benefits for our family.

In July, 1959, we sold our house in Aurora, along with all of our furniture, and traveled westward to California in our 1956 Chevy Nomad with 20-month-old Kenny bouncing on the seat between us. The only furniture item we kept was Cathy's cedar chest which I had given to her as a graduation present. Our intent was to use the free furniture supplied by the U.S. Government for all employees living on the island.

The trip to California took 3 days and was the farthest west either of us had been in our lives. We had serious doubts and apprehension along the way and even contemplated turning the car around and heading back east. On the third day we entered California and there was no turning back. As we finally ascended the Bay Bridge connecting Oakland with San Francisco, we looked northwest and saw the haunting image of a fog-shrouded Alcatraz Island sitting lonely in the middle of the bay. Without hesitation, I turned to Cathy and, with a lump in my throat, said, "What in the hell did we just do??"

CHAPTER THREE

Moving to San Francisco certainly brought about its share of apprehension but, at the same time it also instilled in us a new sense of excitement and provided the ability to make a "fresh start". The loss of a child and family members had driven home the point that life was short and you had to appreciate daily the many blessings given to you. In the grand scheme of things, there was a reason we were being moved 1300 miles away from our home and I was being placed in the most notorious prison in the world. We needed to embrace this new life and all the joys and challenges that came with it.

One of our first challenges came immediately after arriving in the Bay area. Upon accepting the position at Alcatraz, we were told over the phone on our first day in town that there were no island apartment vacancies and it could possibly be several months before anything became available. To make things even more interesting, we had sold all our furniture in Colorado with expectations of being provided free, government-issue furniture in our island apartment.

The month we arrived the Federal Bureau of Prisons decided to put a stop to that practice. I joked that they must've known we were coming!

We checked into a small hotel near Fisherman's Wharf, at our expense, and quickly searched through newspapers for nearby apartments. We placed a red circle on a local map and set out to find something in close proximity to the Alcatraz boat dock at Fort Mason. Rental rates turned out to be VERY expensive compared to what we once paid back in Iowa and ironically, most places would take pets, but not children. After being turned down by a few landlords, we contemplated having Kenny don a fur suit and learn to bark. We soon found a friendly landlord, however, who allowed children and rented a fully furnished two bedroom apartment on a month-to-month basis.

The apartment was located less that one mile from Fort Mason and for an additional fee, the Nomad also moved into its own rental garage just down the street. Unforeseen expenses aside, it felt great to finally get settled and begin focusing on my new job.

I was up bright and early on my Monday start date and dressed sharply in my best suit and tie. I kissed Cathy and Kenny goodbye after breakfast and left them getting settled before walking down the street to catch the 8:20 A.M. boat. Most dayshift employees had left for work an hour earlier on the 7:30 A.M. boat, so this trip would largely be shared with a handful of officers scheduled to start work at 9:00 A.M. and women returning from early morning trips to the grocery store.

While waiting to board the boat I noticed it was difficult to tell between officers and general employees because everyone was in civilian clothes. Officers were not allowed to wear uniforms on the mainland and changed clothing before and after shifts in the officer's locker room located in the lower level of the 64 Building. Only two other people were wearing a suit and tie, so I quickly surmised that these were fellow recruits out for their first day of training.

At 8:15 A.M. we were invited onboard the Warden Johnston by the boat officer who greeted nearly everyone by name as they climbed the gangway. Before the recruits were allowed to board, however, we were required to present our job acceptance letters as a means of identification and the boat officer matched our letters with written names on a clipboard. After showing my paperwork, I was officially greeted with a hearty "Welcome aboard Mr. Albright!" I climbed the plank and found a seat near the bow in somewhat cramped quarters.

At 8:20 A.M. sharp, the boat officer sounded a short blast on the boat's horn and the Warden Johnston pulled away from Fort Mason and out into the Bay. My first trip to Alcatraz started and I became very excited, especially in anticipation of what was ahead.

I was on the left side of the boat and was immediately afforded a spectacular view of the Golden Gate Bridge and adjoining Headlands. I soaked up the scenery as we traveled further out into the bay and a lump began to form in my throat as the 'ROCK" came closer into view. I silently wondered "what in the heck am I doing." What made it even more intriguing was the fact that nearly everyone around me chatted and appeared impervious to my thoughts. Looking across the aisle, I spotted the two other recruits sitting nervously, one wringing his hands, as we awaited our imminent arrival.

As the boat drew within a couple hundred yards of Alcatraz, I was surprised to see how beautiful the grounds surrounding the prison actually looked. From the mainland, Alcatraz appeared cold and foreboding yet, the closer I got, it seemed to come alive with an abundance of flora streaming down the side of the hills. This pleasant sight soon tempered my feeling of uneasiness.

The boat pulled into the dock on the eastern edge of the island and I immediately noticed several inmates in uniform. They were lined up on a painted white line on the dock, near the garage, awaiting the boat's arrival and our departure. Generally, 5 or 6 inmates worked the dock area during daytime hours, Monday through Friday, performing a multitude of tasks. These inmates had to be lined up on the white line before any of the boats could come in or leave. Nevertheless, I must admit that it was somewhat unsettling to have convicts that close, but I guess I needed to get used to it.

Immediately after disembarking, the dock officer gathered the new recruits together and conducted a quick roll call. We were then directed to officially sign-in at the dock office. "Bob", "Joe" and I then boarded the island bus, driven by the dock officer, which would take us up the steep and winding road to the main cellhouse. Looking out the bus window afforded a spectacular view of the bay and, at the same time, a nerve-racking view down the side of Alcatraz's rocky cliffs. There would be more than a few sweaty palms, burnt clutches and worn out brakes experienced over the years traveling these steep grades.

The bus came to a stop near the door of the administration building where we were met by the training officer, Wells Irving. Officer Irving was a seasoned officer in his mid-40s and his military-style, flat-top haircut gave him a commanding presence. Due to a high attrition rate in the Alcatraz officer ranks; he was constantly busy training new officers attracted through an aggressive recruiting campaign by the Federal Bureau of Prisons. Many officers quickly became disenchanted after only a brief exposure to prison life, however, and it became a constant battle to retain people. As I would soon find out, many seasoned officers were less than enthusiastic about spending energy training new officers when they were likely to leave anyway.

Officer Irving was my first on-site trainer. Shortly after my arrival he was transferred and Cecil "Red" Howell, the Assistant Training Officer, became the new Training Officer. He finished my on-site training.

One of the first things I had to do was get my picture taken and be issued a Department of Justice Federal Prison System Identification Card.

Officer Irving directed us into the administration building conference room and dutifully distributed copies of the institution's rules and regulations. These were issued to all officers and inmates and Officer Irving stated "learn these as they must be followed without exception." I immediately began thumbing through the pages and was quickly surprised by the strictness of the prison rules. I began to realize why the prison had such a strong reputation. I didn't know then but it didn't take me long to understand what made Alcatraz different from other federal prisons. It was all about "total control." This total control was applied to every inmate and was strictly enforced throughout the inmate's time on Alcatraz. Inmates were provided very basic rights and everything had to be earned as a privilege. Wells told us that "Alcatraz wasn't a country club like many other prisons and strictness was necessary for retaining law and order." We were told that the rules and regulations are the guide for both guards and inmates, and that we needed to absorb every detail to ensure our personal safety as well as the safety of fellow officers and inmates. The administrative offices, including the offices of the Warden and others were separated from the actual cellhouse which housed the inmates, by a solid wall with a metal door entrance. I kept looking at that door and thinking, "What am I going to see on the other side."

At the conclusion of the rules review, our next stop was a meeting with the prison Warden, Paul Madigan. He was in his fourth year as head of the institution and generally well-respected by employees and even most inmates. He had a reputation as a tough, but fair man, who brought about needed reform to Alcatraz. He greeted each of us with a smile and firm handshake as we filed by his desk. Pictures of President Eisenhower and Federal Bureau of Prisons Chief James Bennett adorned the walls and the smell of Warden Madigan's trademark pipe tobacco wafted around every corner of the room.

Warden Madigan, being relatively political by nature, spoke to us about the excellence of his team and how in a short period of time we would be trained to join the "best of the best" in the U.S. Federal Bureau of Prisons system. He stressed that our jobs were never to be taken lightly, no matter how mundane, and we were expected to maintain a professional, positive demeanor in everything we did. The rules were to be followed, without exception, and any deviation would be grounds for immediate reprimand or even dismissal. The reputation of the prison administration and U. S. Government was at stake every time we stepped behind the iron gates.

By the time our Madigan "pep talk" was finished, we were ready to step into a world few people ever got to see first-hand. Security was extremely tight behind the prison walls and only screened and trained employees were allowed in the inner sanctum.

Visitors, except for those with special permission, were not allowed within the prison. I got my first taste of what to expect when warned that inmates would test us early, and often, in an attempt to see what we were made of and to possibly gain an edge. Although I felt fairly confident that I was ready, I noticed uneasiness in my two fellow trainees.

Officer Irving led us through the administration offices and introduced us to the Associate Warden and Captain of the Guards before heading to the control room located by the main gate. After a brief conversation with the control room officer, the main gate was activated and we stepped inside a holding area between two metal doors. The procedure to enter the cellhouse was straightforward, check-in at the control center, walk a few yards, open a door and stand in a foyer. The main gate officer met you. He would peek into the cellhouse through a bullet resistant window, provide clearance, and then open a thick, steel-reinforced door leading to a final holding area. Once this reinforced door was closed, a final door was opened and you briskly stepped forward into the cellhouse. I had anticipated this ever since my being accepted as a guard and now the time had come as we stepped into the cellhouse. Wild thoughts were racing through my mind, especially as I had no prior experience or training in any prison, Federal or otherwise. "What would it look like?" "Who is actually inside?" "How are the inmates dealt with?" "Where would the inmates be?" "What would they say when they saw us for the first time?" Shortly after stepping into the cellhouse the final door closed with a loud CLANG which echoed throughout the cellhouse. The closing of that final damn door woke me up from my daydreaming and sent a chill up my spine. During my 26-year career with the Federal Bureau of Prisons very few experiences made a more lasting impression than entering the Alcatraz main cellhouse.

Entering the cellhouse often struck me as ironic. One minute you'd be outside admiring the beautiful San Francisco skyline and inhaling ocean breezes. Thirty yards and three metal doors later you entered the domain of murders, rapist, robbers, and hardened criminals.

Nearly every officer's attitude changed once they entered the cellhouse. Outside the Main gate I would joke and have light-hearted conversations with fellow officers. Once I stepped into the inner sanctum, however, everything was serious business and I was ready for action, whatever it may be!

Several features immediately caught my attention. The lights were very bright which created a gleaming effect on the highly polished floors. Inmates mopped and polished floors on a daily basis to the point where you could actually see your silhouette when you looked down. Their mothers would've been proud! Another feature were four rows of cells, stacked 3 high, which stood free-form in the middle of the room without connecting to walls or ceilings. It reminded me of 4 large rows of file cabinets, evenly spaced, in the middle of an office. Natural light poured through windows on either side of the cellhouse complementing the artificial lighting. This combination of lights especially brightened cells facing windows making them highly desirable to inmates. Unfortunately, this affinity towards windows made isolation cells in D-Block strangely desirable. Desperate inmates would even act up on purpose just to get a change of scenery.

The cellhouse was eerily quiet as most inmates were at their job assignments in various locations around the prison and the island. The few inmates that remained cell bound were generally held back due to illness, disciplinary reasons or general refusal to work.

Our footsteps echoed as we walked up and down the aisles between the four cell blocks. Officer Irving pointed out various features of the cells and I was amazed by how tiny and sparse they were. A standard cell was 5 feet wide, 9 feet deep and 7 feet high. Cell doors were operated by a locking mechanism at the end of each block which could unlock cells individually, in a range or in unison. Inside each cell was a bed with a cotton mattress, 2 blankets, a small work table with a folding seat below, and a toilet and wash basin with hot water (prior to 1961 there was only cold water available). A small bookshelf hung on the back wall above the toilet and held an inmate's allotted number of books and magazines. The cells were neat and clean. Many were decorated with pictures and paintings from cellhouse artists and there were even radio jacks for headphones that allowed inmates to listen to selective, prison-censored San Francisco radio stations.

Officer Irving also pointed out that each block was designated alphabetically and walkways in-between had their own nicknames (this will be discussed in more detail later in the book).

As we walked between Cell Blocks C and D, I heard a cat-like "snarling" sound coming from one of the upper tiers. A couple of us looked up and saw a craggy, old inmate with his face pressed to the bars boldly extending his middle finger as if to say "Welcome to Alcatraz, rookies!" We mused that he must've been president of the island "Welcome Wagon" committee.

Officer Irving soon directed us outside where we stood on the upper steps of the stairway leading to the recreation yard. We watched as inmates began returning from their jobs in industries. At the 11:50 A.M. count bell the inmates formed lines according to their cellblocks and galleries and, shortly thereafter, were dismissed by officers to march single-file up the stairs for noon dining in the main dining hall.

At this point we were dismissed for our lunch break and I chose to retreat to the employee break room near the administrative officers while my two fellow recruits followed Officer Irving to the culinary area in the back of the dining hall. I wasn't quite ready to partake of inmate-prepared food and found Cathy's lunch to be a welcome alternative.

CHAPTER FOUR

I thought a lot about the initial introduction to the cellhouse and the inmates. Excitement, anticipation and the unknown all raced through my mind as I finished lunch. Officer Irving brought me back to the kitchen where he left me with the Officer-in-charge of clean-up duty. I started to realize that the orientation was over and my training was about to begin. Joe went to the clothing room and Bob to the west gun gallery.

The inmates working in the kitchen went about their chores rinsing silverware, trays and cups before placing them in the industrial size dishwasher. Larger items such as pots and pans had to be washed by hand in a nearby sink. All leftover food, paper and other disposables were placed in large barrels and were carried out and burned in the incinerator on the west end of the island.

The officer in charge stressed paying particular attention to how the inmates handled silverware as these items could easily be smuggled and turned into weaponry. Most interesting were the helpful tips about interacting with inmates and pitfalls to avoid when they tried to "test" a new guard. He stated, "They'll try every trick in the book to swindle, cheat, and lie." It didn't take long before I found this out first-hand.

Shortly thereafter, I was alone in the back room of the bakery/kitchen observing the inmates going about their chores when several of them, standing very close to me, struck up a conversation about Camel cigarettes. "Those Camels sure beat this Bull Durham crap they've got in stock here" said Gilford (AZ 926). "Yeah, I remember the good old days when we were kids and smoked them Camels. They sure was a good smoke."

"Any of em up there on that shelf?" asked another con.

"Naw, unfortunately they're all out of them," responded Gilford.

Upon hearing this conversation, I remembered that my own pack of Camels was visible from my shirt pocket. These guys were no dummies and, indirectly, were asking me to part with my smokes. If I hadn't been warned, I might've broken down and slipped them the pack. They seemed like nice enough guys, but that was all part of the game. I wasn't going to compromise myself by falling into their trap and losing my job. I later learned that Camels were not issued to the inmates as they were issued Wing cigarettes and Bull Durham tobacco to roll their own.

After clean-up was over, Joe, Bob and I re-convened and spent the remainder of the day touring and observing several spots on the island including the hospital, gun galleries, recreation yard, industries shops, incinerator and greenhouse. The inmates afforded us more than a few dirty looks and under-the-breath comments. Officer Irving casually told us to ignore them. There were very few times in my life where I felt more hated by a group of people; except, perhaps when I tied the inner tube to my car's exhaust pipe – but that's another story.

At 4:00 P.M. we boarded the bus outside the administration building and proceeded to the dock for our boat ride to Fort Mason and home. While making our circuitous journey down the steep road, I watched some women and children walking on the Parade Ground toward their living quarters, Building 64. I immediately thought of Cathy and Kenny and dreamed of the day when my trip home would only consist of a short walk down the hill to an island apartment. Taking walks, watching the ships pass in the harbor or playing catch on the Parade Ground seemed distant and my thoughts were soon interrupted as we arrived at the dock.

Joe, Bob and I made small talk as we waited for the 4:30 P.M. boat to arrive. They were local Bay area men who also had no prior prison work experience and were lured by radio ads for government jobs promising good pay and benefits. We laughed that we hadn't seen any of that yet and that there were probably easier ways to make a living. They half-jokingly said I was "crazy" for moving over 1000 miles to work at Alcatraz. I laughed, but deep down, wondered if they weren't right.

Soon we boarded the boat and were on our way. I was deep in thought as we chopped across the waves to Fort Mason. Had I made the right decision? Was I really cut-out to deal with hate-filled and violent criminals on a daily basis? Would Cathy be happy in the strange new environment? The questions were numerous and only time would bear the truth.

I arrived home at the apartment to find Cathy and Kenny playing in the sparsely equipped living room. Cathy had things well organized and the place looked pretty "homey." To celebrate my first official day on Alcatraz, we took a leisurely stroll to Fisherman's Wharf and ate at one of the many seafood restaurants. Everything was fresh and excellent, unlike the seafood back home which was shipped frozen and had a certain "mushiness" to it after thawing.

Cathy spoke glowingly about the great park near the apartment where she took Kenny. It was within walking distance and afforded a great view of the bay. In addition to the things to keep kids occupied, she met other mothers who befriended her. My concerns about her happiness in San Francisco quickly began to fade.

In answer to Cathy's many questions about my first day on the island, I spoke enthusiastically about the first boat trip and soaking up the spectacular scenery. I described how beautiful Alcatraz actually was up close with its abundance of flowers and creeping vegetation covering the sandstone cliffs. Even the buildings had a certain architectural beauty, especially the warden's residence and the lighthouse. I also described the many friendly prison staff and guards that I had met and how helpful they were during my orientation. I neglected to mention, however, the various inmate snarls and catcalls we received throughout the day. There was no sense in spoiling the positive mood of the evening. To cap off our evening meal, we stopped for some fresh Ghirardelli's chocolate ice cream.

My second day was in sharp contrast with the first. There was no need for identification while boarding the boat as I was immediately recognized and waved onboard with a hearty welcome. Visibility in the bay was extremely poor this morning as a thick fog had rolled in overnight and blanketed the entire Bay area. Foghorns could be heard droning from the Golden Gate Headlands to the west and from Alcatraz to the east.

I became a little unsettled as we pulled away from Fort Mason and literally couldn't see more than a few yards beyond the boat. How in the world could the boat officer see an oncoming freighter and react in time in this pea-soup fog? To top it off, a seasoned officer at the Fort Mason dock told us that the Warden Johnston was NOT equipped with modern radar and relied mainly upon the "lookout" method of navigating. After hearing these reassuring words, Joe and Bob appeared even more nervous than the previous morning.

As we drew closer to Alcatraz, the foghorns, which alternatively blasted from the north and south ends of the island at 30-second intervals, grew louder and louder. The fog had lifted slightly as we drew within a couple hundred yards of the shore and a mysterious image of the island began to appear through the mist. There was no beauty in this arrival, only a dull grayness that seemed befitting of Alcatraz's lore and mystique.

The dock officer met us and offered congratulations on surviving our first foggy boat trip. We were not required to sign in at the dock office this morning, but were taken to the officer's locker room, located in the basement of the 64 Building. Once inside, we were given a lock and assigned a locker. Next we were fitted with a wardrobe of officer's clothing – 1 cap, 1 belt, 2 uniform coats, 1 overcoat, 1 pair of trousers, 3 shirts and 2 pair of shoes. We were told that we would be supplied with 2 pair of shoes every 18 months. (I still have my original hat, whistle, and uniform, except for the jacket.) It was emphasized that guards were not allowed to wear their uniforms off the island.

Roll call was at 8:00 A.M., in front of the administration building, and we hurriedly changed so we wouldn't be late. Everything seemed to fit pretty well, although I hated wearing the hat. In subsequent weeks, I would quickly remove the hat after arriving at my designated post.

When we arrived a line of officers had already formed and we quickly joined them. I was one of the first names read by the officer-in-charge, Lieutenant Maurice Ordway. Lieutenant Ordway was nicknamed "Double Tough" for his "tough-as-nails" disposition and aggressive enforcement of prison rules. Nobody messed with him and I gulped as he briskly inspected my uniform and introduced me to the other officers. "Gentlemen, this is James Albright who has moved from Englewood, Colorado, to join our officer's ranks." There was no applause or movement as the other officers stood firmly in line at attention. Only after he had moved well down the line did a friendly officer beside me say "Welcome Aboard, Albright."

After receiving instructions we were dismissed from roll call. Officer Irving took us to the meeting room and handed each of us a personalized one-year on-the-job training schedule. I had been deeply concerned about what type training I would receive, especially as I had no prior experience, at all, in any form of law enforcement. I felt more relaxed after meeting with Officer Irving and receiving and discussing my detailed training schedule. Also I became even more excited about what lay ahead and began to feel that I would soon be getting exposure to what makes Alcatraz's brutal reputation.

My first 32 weeks of training would consist of orientation and one-day "on-the-job" training posts with the remaining time consisting of eleven, one month on-the-job "departmental" training posts. The training schedule was a guide only as guards could and would be sent to other areas as needed. This occurred quite frequently during my training schedule. The training schedule pointed out

"Stand roll call in front of Administration Building. Above posts are scheduled from 8:00 A.M. to 4:30 P.M., except 'Morning Watch', which is from Midnight to 8:00 A.M., and the 'Evening Watch', which is 4:00 P.M. to Midnight."

The on-the-job training sessions required spending one day "shadowing" an officer. Here we would learn the rules and procedures of the position. The one-month departmental training posts would give us more of a "hands on" opportunity to put what we learned to practice in real-life conditions with the "safety net" of an accompanying officer. By the time our year of training was finished, we would essentially be exposed to every officer position around the entire island.

Depending on the post assigned, as an armed guard, we would carry a .38 caliber pistol, carbine, 30.06 rifle, gas gun, or a gas billy. Needless to say, one instruction that was clearly communicated to all the guards was the authorized use of firearms. Guns and tear gas were only to be used as a "last resort." In a memorandum submitted to all armed officers, Captain Emil Rychner wrote:

"This memorandum is submitted to clarify any questions that any employee may have in when and under what conditions the use of firearms is authorized.

Personnel will be authorized to use firearms only as a last resort to prevent escapes, protect government property, and to prevent injury or loss of life of personnel or inmates who are held hostage.

Orders to halt or to desist will first be given and if not complied with, a warning shot will be fired. Should the inmate continue in his effort to escape, destroy vital government property, or to endanger the lives of personnel, or inmate hostages, firearms shall be used in an effort to disable rather than kill.

Tear gas and gas guns will only be used on the order of the Warden."

E. E. Rychner, Captain

The handling of guns on Alcatraz was very serious business, especially following the shootings of 3 officers during the 1946 riots. Toy guns were forbidden for use by island children. In a document that laid out regulations for island residents, the following rules applied for firearms and ammunition:

"These (firearms and ammunition) are our greatest hazard. Personal firearms and ammunition must be kept in the Control Center. Toy pistols and guns, under certain conditions could be as dangerous as the real thing, and they, along with fire crackers. etc., are not permitted on the island.

Weapons or ammunition should never be sent directly to the island. Make arrangements to pick them up in San Francisco at the express or freight office. When you wish to bring them to the island, notify the captain and make necessary arrangements well ahead of time."

Warden Madigan outlined a violation of the toy gun rule in a letter to residents on November 23, 1960, which read in part:

"It was very disturbing to me and other members of the staff to find that within the past few days an inmate was found in possession of a very life-like, but toy pistol. This item came out of the trash or garbage from island residents. It hardly seems necessary that I should point out the many and varied hazards of such an incident. Fortunately the pistol was disposed of immediately and was not used in an escape attempt where lives could very well have been lost...."

CHAPTER FIVE

With a comprehensive training schedule in hand and a good understanding about the carrying of weapons, I was told that my first on-the-job training post would be Tower #1, near the boat dock. Joe and Bob would be posted to the hospital and kitchen respectively.

Officer Irving took several hours to brief us on certain procedures and various "shakedown" methods.

First, each guard position on the island had a job analysis sheet which was available in the Captain's office. The job sheets were generally between 2 and 5 pages long and were small enough to fit neatly inside the pocket of an officer's coat. Details of each post were provided including tasks and times for specific duties. These sheets outlined the major events and times to guide the officer in performing his duties. Additionally, each officer was required to always carry a watch, pencil, notebook and whistle for all job assignments. During the hours of darkness, guards were also required to carry a flashlight.

We were told that everybody on the 6 P.M. to 6 A.M. shifts were required to make "watch calls" to the control center. This constituted dialing the numbers "333" every half-hour to give our location. The guard in the hospital was required to call every 15 minutes as he was less protected in that area. Missing a call was a "no-no" and each officer had a system to make sure he didn't miss the call. Some would write times down and then check them off or write they called. In Tower #2, a special board called the "TWEETY" board was used. This board was designed by Officer Gene Glaum, thus he got the nickname "Tweety." It was a board with peg holes representing every 30 minutes from 6 P.M. to 6 A.M. The times were written next to each hole and the guard would move the peg after he called to the hole representing that time. This allowed the guard to look and insure he made the call and also tell when the next call was due.

Inmates were notorious for concealing contraband and had to be scrutinized at every turn. Everything from homemade knives, hooch (alcohol), illegal cigarettes, gum and explosive materials could be found during shakedowns of inmates and their cells. Metal detectors were a partial deterrent, but the "cons" always seemed to find a way to bypass the machines thus requiring serious hand checking.

We were instructed on the right and wrong ways to question and shake-down inmates. We were told to be firm and direct in our questioning which, if done properly, might flush out contraband and avoid shakedowns altogether. When shakedowns were unavoidable, every part of the body needed to be inspected and modesty was not in the vocabulary during these events. In many cases, inmates were asked to strip and the Medical Technician Assistant's (MTA) fingers were placed where the sun didn't shine.

After this briefing we were sent to our assignments. I grabbed my lunch from the administration break room before starting the down hill walk to Tower #1. A secretary in the administration building suggested that I take the stairway behind the doctor's residence as a short-cut down the hill. The stairs were very steep and I was glad to have the assistance of a hand-railing.

As I approached Tower #1, the question came to mind; "How was I going to let the officer in the Tower know I had arrived?" Would I need to stand at the bottom and yell loudly to get his attention? Would it require jumping around and waving my arms? Luckily, he was already anticipating my arrival as the Control Center officer had radioed my departure from the main gate and he had spotted me making the arduous journey down the hill. A friendly wave and yell "c'mon up" was all I needed to begin my climb skyward.

Tower #1 was an impressive structure and one of the tallest free-standing prison towers built. It was nearly 50 feet tall and offered a birds-eye view of the entire dock area, 64 Building, East Bay and the hill leading up to the cellhouse. As I climbed the long ladder, I felt the mist of the dissipating fog swirling around me and watched as a seagull flew by me at eye-level. The tower door was already open when I reached the last set of stairs to enter the tower.

The tower officer, George Black, was very friendly and seemed genuinely happy to have me join him in his dockside perch. After all, sitting by yourself in a tower for 8 hours was bound to get rather monotonous and lonely. Officer Black showed me the various features of the tower including the radio, the telephone for dialing the "deuces", or "222", if there was an emergency, and the potty for when nature called. He also showed me his binoculars and high-powered rifle which never left the tower while prisoners were working at the dock.

Tower #1 was one of the most important towers on the island as it monitored daily boat arrivals and departures and kept a watchful eye on inmates working the dock area. It also provided an entertaining view of civilian life as people came and went from 64 Building and the island bus dropped off, and picked up, passengers near its base. People were constantly waving skyward and quite often you were close to eye level with residents walking on the upper balconies of 64 Building. With the exception of Tower #4, Tower #1 was easily exposed to the most daily activity on the island.

After a couple hours, our conversation turned away from business and focused on more personal subjects. I explained how I looked forward to the day when my family would live in 64

Building thereby eliminating my daily commute and high rent on the mainland. Officer Black had two young children who attended elementary school in San Francisco and they commuted daily on the Warden Johnston.

The arrival of the 3 P.M. boat was always interesting because it marked the return of island children from the mainland schools. Although every boat was treated with importance, the children were watched extra carefully as they made their way toward 64 Building or to board the bus heading to the A-B-C apartments on the western edge of the Parade Ground past inmates who were required to stand on the white line until all were cleared. Children were always encouraged to leave the dock area immediately and were not allowed to enter that area until 10 minutes prior to a boat departure when the boat horn was sounded.

Officer Black moved out next to the railing as a group of children made their way toward the island bus. A couple of elementary-aged girls waved up at the tower and screamed, "Hi, daddy!" Officer Black waved back and smiled before they yelled another question up to him.

"Who's that up in your 'nest' daddy?" the youngest daughter asked. "This is Officer Albright, he's brand new and I'm just teaching him a few things," George replied. "Did you show him your gun?" asked the oldest. "Yes, I did," George replied nervously while looking over at the prisoners. "I'll see you at supper." "Ok, daddy. See you later!"

"Kids, they're something else," Officer Black said to me with a smile. I was amused by the exchange and once again looked forward to the day when Cathy and Kenny would join me on the island.

Day 2 ended with a walk down the ladder and a quick change in the locker room before catching the 4:30 P.M. boat. I thought about all the things I had learned and done in the last two days. Joe and Bob joined me and we compared notes about our first full day of training sessions. I spoke positively about being in Tower #1. "Sounds like you had a more eventful day than mine" I said. "Things were pretty quiet after a couple hours in the kitchen and it got boring" said Bob. Joe replied, "I was exposed to those 'loony toons' up in the hospital. Couldn't believe it, but there were some guys who had just cut their heel tendons on purpose. Are those guy's nuts or what? Why in the world would we want to work in a place where they're doing stuff like that?" Poor Joe, I thought to myself. It won't be long before he's heading back to the mainland for employment.

My third day was fast-paced as they had me hopping between Towers #2, 3, 4 and 5. Tower #2 was located near the road, #3 at the water tower, #4 on top the old industries building and Tower #5 on the ground by the back side of the kitchen basement. There was also a Tower #6 on the cellhouse roof which was no longer manned and was removed a few months after my arrival. There was a mixed bag of personalities as the officers in #2 and #4 took the time to train me properly while #3 was ambivalent and #5 seemed rather hostile. In fact, the officer in Tower #5 said to me shortly after I joined him, "I don't know why I'm spending time training you guys. In a few weeks you'll be back over in San Francisco doing something else. We need to get some seasoned vets from other prisons in here so we aren't constantly churning through greenhorns."

Upon hearing the officer's remarks I silently boiled over the fact that I was being categorized with the other "quitters" who had preceded me. Yeah, I wasn't sure this was something I wanted to do for the rest of my life but, for the time being, I was going to work hard and give it my best shot. After all, too much time and energy had been devoted in uprooting my family and I wasn't about to turn around and leave now.

At the end of Day #3, the three rookies conducted a now-customary comparing of notes. As it turned out, Bob had a very interesting day working with the officer in the main control center which prompted me to look forward to that rotation in week #3. Joe, on the other hand, had another dismal day. "I'm training with this guy Lewis down in the clothing room and the first thing he does is throw the rule book at me and say 'Here, read this.'" I asked him a couple questions and his answers were real short or indistinguishable grunts. So, basically, I sat there for 7 hours in a damp basement staring at a bunch of towels and getting the silent treatment from this jerk." I wondered who had a worse attitude, Lewis or Joe.

My next rotation, day #4, took me back down to the dock. This time, however, I was at ground-level working with the friendly dock officer who had greeted us throughout the week. Compared to the relative idleness of the towers, the dock was a hub of activity with boat passengers every half hour, loading and unloading of barges and 5 inmates to keep an eye on. The inmates working at the dock were among the more trusted and earned their positions through good conduct. They still had to be watched especially when dealing with civilians, which included women, children and visitors. Once again, I was put to the test.

"First time working' the dock?" asked an inmate as he hoisted a bag of flour from the island barge and placed in on a cart.

"Yes," I responded in a cool manner."

"Don't suppose you want to part with that cigar in your pocket." He asked shyly.

"No, now get back to work!" I responded abruptly surprising him and, frankly, myself. Our conversation ended immediately and he re-focused on lifting items off the barge. At this point I realized I was learning some valuable lessons. First, keep all personal belongings out of the sight of inmates to avoid unnecessary temptation. Even little things like cigarettes, cigars and candy had value behind prison walls and inmates would try every trick in the book to weasel them away from you. Secondly, showing an authoritative voice and strong presence would reduce future temptations.

"What's going on over there?" asked the dock officer who heard my raised voice. "Oh, just telling this guy to get back to work," I responded. I could've prosecuted the inmate by telling the dock officer, but figured it was my own naivety that led to the encounter in the first place. Asking officers for personal items was a serious offense and could potentially result in loss of good time and, possibly, a highly prized dock job. I wasn't ready to make my first inmate enemy at this point and used an officer's judgment to let things slide. Every day would be a judgment test regarding rule violations.

My final day in the first week was in the clothing room which was located in the basement near the inmate showers. I had been forewarned about Officer Lewis, the clothing room supervisor, and found him to be nearly as unpleasant as Joe had described. I was given the rule book and told to sit in a chair on the opposite side of the cage. I was very proactive with my questions, however, and Officer Lewis seemed to warm up a bit near the end of my rotation. Perhaps he could see that I was serious about staying and had a real interest in learning his position.

Our end-of-week dockside discussion was rather telling as I spoke about how Alcatraz wasn't so bad and how I thought I could stick it out. The fear and apprehension of the first couple days had quickly subsided and given way to a new sense of purpose and self-fulfillment. Bob half-heartedly agreed, but still had reservations on whether this was in his long-term plans. Joe, however, was pretty adamant that Alcatraz was a "rotten" institution and wondered aloud whether this was the right job for him. Bob and I both suggested that life was too short to be miserable and he might be better suited to find a job which made him happier. He nodded and remained quiet until we parted at the boat dock. "Maybe I'll see you guys on Monday but, if not, it was nice meeting both of you," were Joe's parting comments. I waved good-bye and wished him a good weekend and, under my breath, best wishes in his future endeavors.

Cathy and Kenny had walked down to meet me at the Fort Mason boat dock and we went grocery shopping at the Safeway store across the street. Cathy had met several of the officer's wives at the checkout counter earlier in the week and found them to be very pleasant. The store clerks, however, seemed to be wary of Alcatraz people. The local press did its best to sensationalize prison personnel, so perception became reality among San Franciscans. Alcatraz officers, in particular, were regarded as a tough group and looked upon with a certain sense of fear and suspicion. After all, officers supposedly beat and tortured everyone in sight including prisoners, wives, small children, dogs, cats and ESPECIALLY, store clerks! If they only knew we were just docile employees trying to make a living, perhaps they'd have changed their tune.

CHAPTER SIX

San Francisco offered a lot of opportunities and things to do. We spent our first open weekend traveling across the Golden Gate to visit Muir Woods and Stinson Beach. We stopped at a roadside turnout near the northern end of the Golden Gate Bridge and were afforded a spectacular view of the bridge and the San Francisco skyline. Alcatraz sat lonely in the middle of the bay from this vantage point reinforcing its aura of inescapability. We quickly warmed up to San Francisco and became enamored with its uniqueness. There were a combination of sights and sounds you couldn't experience anywhere else in the world. Cable and trolley cars clanging, foghorns droning, ships signaling, seals barking and horns honking provided a medley of sounds rarely heard in one setting. The "big" things such as boats, bridges, buses and huge hills really impressed Kenny. He was also greatly amused by the antics of the silly seals at Seal Rock.

After packing as much enjoyment as possible into one weekend, I arrived at the Fort Mason dock on Monday morning of my second week with a new sense of excitement about San Francisco and anticipation about my new job. As I sat and waited to board the Warden Johnston, Bob walked over and sat down on the bench next to me.

"Seen Joe this morning?" I asked.

"Nope, I'll lay odds he's a goner," replied Bob.

"I think you're right. We're only 5 minutes away from boarding and he's usually here by now," I replied.

A quick blast from the boat horn told us it was time to board and we made our way down the stairs across the platform and onto the pitching boat. I kept a watchful eye out the window only half expecting to see Joe tearing towards the boat in a last-minute frenzy. His fate was sealed, however, as we pulled away from Fort Mason out into the Bay.

Roll call confirmed Joe's absence as Lieutenant Ordway walked down the row of officers and read through the list of names. "Englehardt, Evans, Farren, Fowler...Anyone seen Fowler this morning?" growled Lieutenant Ordway. "I believe he has left us," replied Bob from further down the line. Lieutenant Ordway shook his head and snapped, "As a reminder to you new guys, you need to call the dock office if you plan to be absent from work! We are assuming Fowler has left us but, if he shows up tomorrow with an unexplained absence, there will be hell to pay!" You could feel the tension in the group and I glanced down the row to see more than a few Adam's apples going up and down. God forbid tomorrow's roll call if Joe showed and had to face the wrath of Lieutenant Ordway.

Before the start of each shift, guards were required to line-up for inspection and roll call either in front of the administration building in good weather or inside if raining. The inspection was conducted by the Lieutenant of the shift and included ensuring that shoes were shined, uniforms cleaned and pressed, hats appropriately worn, and faces cleanly shaven. As noted previously, I did not like wearing my hat and I would normally either put it in my locker after the inspection or remove it after arriving at my designated post. The Lieutenant would give any special instructions or advice on particulars such as last night one of the inmates was restless in his cell or an inmate may have threatened someone, etc. As soon as inspection was over we went to our assigned area.

Officer Irving was noticeably disappointed when only Bob and I arrived at his office. Fortunately, he had only invested a week in training Joe as opposed to other officers who left after spending months going through the process. Turnover was an inherent risk of a training officer's job.

My training assignment for the second week included the hospital, kitchen, west gun gallery, industries and work area. In customary fashion, Officer Irving escorted Bob and me to our assignments. The hospital covered a large section of the second floor on the north side of the prison and was attainable by entering a stairway in the hallway which led to the main dining room. Officer Irving introduced me to the officer in charge and departed with Bob back down the stairs.

"I suppose the first thing you wanna see up here is the Birdman," the officer said wryly.

"Well, I"

"Seems like that's all the rookies wanna see. Well, I hate to disappoint you, but he left last month – flew the coop! We were all glad to see the nasty SOB leave. C'mon, let's go start our tour at the bird cage."

Indeed, Robert Stroud (AZ 594), the infamous Birdman of Alcatraz, had left the island one month prior to my arrival. Yes, I was disappointed yet interested as I heard stories about him a long time before coming to Alcatraz, and my interest was high. Although I never had the opportunity to meet him in person, I did hear many horror stories about this most charming person, from both guards and inmates, none of which were good.

"In case you were wondering, he never had any of those crazy birds here at Alcatraz. The only place that allowed him to have birds was Leavenworth. The only fowl we had up here was the foul odor of his rotten carcass," the officer retorted vindictively. Stroud's hospital cell was nearly four times larger than an average prison cell. It was the same as all the other cells with a steel barred door; however, because of his continuous tirades, a wooden door with a small Plexi-glass window was built over the barred door. This was because the staff and inmates did not want to be harassed by his constant gibberish and foul language and wouldn't have to listen to him blabber on and on. For many years he had been deprived the use of a toilet and was required to use a bedpan until a toilet was installed a couple years prior to his departure. His cell was stark and consisted of only basic amenities including a bed, toilet, sink and shelf for personal belongings. While on Alcatraz he had no special privileges nor was he respected or liked by either the inmates or the administration. As both inmates and guards told me, "Stroud was a royal pain in the ass and he drove us nuts as he would talk constantly and never shut up." He arrived on Alcatraz in 1942 and was transferred to the Medical Center for Federal prisoners in Springfield, Missouri, on July 12, 1959. Stroud died, at the age of 73, of natural causes on November 21, 1963, while in prison at this Center. In total, the "Birdman" spent 17 years of his imprisoned life on Alcatraz, with almost all of this time in segregation, either in D-Block (Cell 42) – 6 years – or in the prison hospital (his last 11 years). The time he spent in segregation in the hospital was due to his failing health. Stroud was separated from the other inmates because of his violent and weird behavior. I am sure he heard of the closing of Alcatraz before his death and I wish I knew his thoughts. All in all, he spent 54 years behind bars with approximately 43 years of his life in solitary confinement. The "Birdman of Alcatraz" was made famous in a movie starring Burt Lancaster. I thought, many times about this man, and what his earlier years must have been like and what a miserable life overall he must have spent on the face of this earth. His reputation as "The Birdman" occurred at Leavenworth Penitentiary in Kansas where he began keeping, studying and publishing books on birds. While in Leavenworth he was given the necessary supplies to attract birds and provide them with feedings. However, from what I was told, not all of the bird seed went to the birds but instead he used it to make (Mash) alcohol in his toilet. That way when he was "shaken down" he would just flush the evidence. At the Federal Prison in Marion, Illinois, an inmate who was an orderly in segregation at the Springfield, Missouri Medical Center when Stroud was there, told me that Stroud asked him "if he had ever eaten anyone." He told me he told Stroud "I am not a Homo." Stroud told him "That is not what I meant." The inmate also told me that Stroud once grabbed him by the arm when he was serving Stroud his meal and said "I meant physically eating a person." He replied to Stroud "You are a degenerate. Don't get near me." Before I close the chapter on Stroud I found it very interesting that there is a Congressional Record – Senate July 25, 1962, on Stroud. I found it very interesting reading.

The officer then directed me into the room next door where an employee was stocking medicine bottles behind a long wooden counter. It reminded me of an old-time drugstore I once frequented back in Iowa. "Here's our pharmacy. Got almost everything you need to cure your ills. Inmates line up daily for the stuff we've got up here. The prison doctor is always prescribing things like aspirin, sleeping pills, cough medicine, etc. Yellow jackets seem to be the most popular 'cause they help the boys to sleep amidst the nightly snoring, coughing, sneezing and farting going on in the cellhouse." "How does the doctor know if they really need the stuff?" I asked inquisitively. "Half the time they don't, but we gotta take 'em for their word on the lighter stuff. It's the officer's job to stand there and make sure they swallow it, otherwise they might try to save it and OD at a later date."

"Speaking of OD'ing, the ol' Birdman pulled that stunt on us a few years back. Seems he was taking his gall bladder medicine and coughing it up after we left. He saved enough pills to kill a horse and, if it weren't for a sharp officer who saw his labored breathing, he'd be long dead by now. They even found his last will and testament stuffed in a tube up his butt. It's going to be your job to pluck one of those suckers out of somebody some day." I could tell the officer was trying to get a reaction out of me, but I'd have no part of it "Got to do what you got to do," I replied. "OK, here are the strip cells for when they really go bonkers; nothing but cold yellow tiles and a hole in the floor for a crapper. We usually put guys in here after they've gone nuts in the dark hole. Sometimes we have to leave 'em in straight jackets so they won't hurt themselves.

They're usually at the end of their rope by the time they make it in here. "Anybody been in here lately?" I inquired. "Funny you should ask. We've got a couple of characters over in the holding cells across from the operating room who visited these cells after cutting their heel tendons,. They were getting desperate down in D-Block and decided to pull a crazy stunt just to get a change of scenery. We temporarily patched 'em, put 'em in the strip cells, and then called the surgeon from the mainland to come over and sew 'em back up. They should be right back in D-Block by sometime tomorrow." What they were attempting to get away from backfired and they now have sore feet. Later I saw one of the inmates who was up on the second tier of segregation going to get a shower. He was hopping as hard and fast as he could down the stairs. Someone had said something about him moving fast. He heard something about someone being kicked down the stairs. I never saw or heard about anyone being kicked down any stairs.

"Here's our x-ray room where we find broken bones and even pictures of stuff they've swallowed. The stomach pump usually does a good job of extracting foreign objects. Guys in the hospital are usually too sick to make it all the way down to the showers, so we give them a bar of soap, a rubber duckie, and throw 'em in that bathtub over there. It's your job to scrub their hairy backs and towel 'em off before throwing them back in their cells. Think you can handle that?" "Uh, yeah." "Speaking of the heel cutters, here's our friends. How ya feelin' boys? Why don't you stand up and do a little dance for our new friend, Mr. Albright!" "Shut the hell up ya no good bull!" screamed the younger of the two cons. "These guys have a 'tendon-see' to lack a sense of humor," quipped the officer as we walked away. "All kidding aside, Jim you don't want to make these guys your enemies. You piss off the wrong guy and next thing you know he's throwing feces at you, or sticking you with a sharp object. I've seen officers push guys to the brink and they always find a way of getting them back. Just don't insult their dignity." "Thanks for the advice. My motto is 'tough but fair,'" I replied with a spur of the moment matter-of-factness usually reserved for a seasoned vet. "I think you're gonna be all right, Albright." This was one of the most informative and educational one day on-the-job training posts and opened my eyes a lot.

Tuesday morning confirmed Joe's departure as we pulled away from the Fort Mason dock without him. I silently wondered whether he missed any part of his weeklong Alcatraz experience; the boat ride, the view from outside the administration building, or commiserating with his newfound buddies down by the dock. At least he could tell people at parties that he had been an officer on Alcatraz, even for a week.

I spent the day on culinary assignment watching inmates clean up breakfast then prepare and serve lunch. I still felt uneasy eating inmate-prepared food, but finally got daring and ate a meal of fried chicken, mashed potatoes and green beans in the small room at the back of the kitchen. Upon realizing there were no razor blades or poison in the food, I happily went back for a second helping. Food on Alcatraz was usually very good and inmates were allowed to take all they could eat within the allotted time, but had to eat all they took. Good food kept inmates happy and some would argue, even softened them up. Near-riot conditions would arise when food took a turn for the worse and usually ended up in the dismissal or reprimand of the head cook.

On Wednesday I stood watch over the cellhouse from the vantage point of the west gun gallery. It was here in 1946 that prisoners climbed up and, using bar spreaders, gained access to the gallery and over-powered the guard on duty. Following this deadly riot, a metal cyclone fence was placed over the bars in an effort to deter such attacks.

The west gun gallery served not only as a key vantage point for observing the cellhouse, but also acted as a back-up position in case of a riot in the dining room. Under riot conditions the dining room gun cage officer could deploy tear gas canisters located in the ceiling. The control center officer would issue gas masks to the dining room guards. Additionally, in the case of a dining room lock-down, keys would be lowered by string from the gun gallery to lock the hallway doors connecting the main cellhouse and corridor leading to the dining area.

By the time I finished my training day in the gun gallery, I realized that this position required a level of alertness and judgment like few others on the island. The gun gallery officer had the ability to use a gas gun and if handled improperly, could quickly place fellow officers' lives in danger. This position was not for beginners or the faint of heart!

My next training posts involved spending two days in the prison industries and work areas. Working in industries was a "privilege" for the inmates and most of them looked forward to working as a way to break up the monotony of everyday prison life. Industries consisted of 6 main shops including: laundry, clothing, tailor, glove, brush and furniture refinishing. Immediately after breakfast on weekdays inmates lined up in the recreation yard on designated yellow lines according to work post and, after going through a count, marched single file down a steep hill, through a metal detector and into their respective work areas.

Work crews were in the process of upgrading and relocating the various shops within the two-story industries building during my training. The institutional laundry, now located on the first floor, was one of the largest in the federal penitentiary system and had recently taken over the space allotted to the former brush shop. The clothing shop moved to the second floor and the number of sewing machines increased to nearly 70 in the new larger location. The tailor and brush shops also moved upstairs and the glove and furniture re-finishing shops filled the first floor space formerly occupied by the clothing, tailor and brush shops.

My next one day on-the-job training was in the cellhouse. Training in the cellhouse for a day allowed me to try my hand at a wide variety of tasks and was a rotation where prison job analysis sheets proved to be very useful.

Cellhouse officers were involved with everything from supervising prison maintenance workers to censoring prisoner mail. Given the age of the facilities, there was always a parade of tradesmen such as plumbers and electricians that needed to be escorted and supervised while working in the dark service corridors between each cellblock. It was in these dark corridors that 3 inmates were killed during the

1946 riots by marines who dropped hand grenades through holes they chopped in the roof.

Cellhouse tasks were assigned based upon the area you were working. For example, officers working the west gun gallery would also be responsible for ringing a bell and opening the recreational yard door so inmates could line up for work call. Officers on B-Block on the west end would be responsible for supervising sick call and standing guard at mess while inmates ate. Officers also had standard tasks such as conducting prisoner counts and keeping a close eye on prisoner movements. Rubber hammers were used during routine checks to detect whether cell bars had a different "ring" due to inmates cutting them.

Following the cellhouse training, the control center was next. This area proved to be one of my favorite training rotations. There was rarely a dull moment as the control center acted as a "nerve center" for everything happening on the island. All firearms and ammunition had to be checked in and out of the control center. Keys to every lock on the island were also kept on 24-hour guard. Radio contacts with every guard tower, dock office and island boats were handled from here. When the Warden's secretary couldn't answer telephone calls, they were re-routed to the control center switchboard. A day spent here flew by quickly and I knew immediately that this would be a place to seek a long-term rotation.

The two days following my control center duty were split between the morning watch (midnight to 8 AM) and evening watch (4 P.M. to midnight). Normally, officers would not work "back-to-back" shifts in this manner but, for two days I was willing to put up with an upheaval in my sleep schedule just so I could learn the ropes. Trainee "watch" shifts were generally "hour-to-hour" which required movement between several posts during an entire 8-hour period. My hourly rotations included several towers, main gate and back into the cellhouse.

Upon returning to the dock at the end of my midnight shift, I was surprised to see a different boat waiting in the slip normally occupied by the venerable Warden Johnston. An old Army "T-Boat" was pinch-hitting today while the Warden Johnston was placed in dry dock to undergo annual repairs and have a new, taller pilothouse installed. Visibility from the old pilothouse was often restricted on stormy days due to spray from waves crashing over the bow. The taller pilothouse, soon coupled with modern radar, afforded greater safety to its occupants.

The one day training sessions went by quickly and gave me a good taste of what lay ahead. In the initial training most of the guards were helpful whereas a few just threw the book at me and said "read these". I was shown how prisoners make knives and guns out of pipes, bar spreaders, and a pipe with a piece of rubber on it that, when hooked up to an air compressor and the prisoner's fingers moved a certain way, imitated oral sex.

I watched carefully and observed closely all the officers. This is how I strengthened my learning. I noticed some guards who were not at all ambitious and a bit on the lazy side and wondered why they were there. Several of the guards I felt were strong and pretty sharp and I observed them and what and how they did things. From these individuals I picked up some strong points and tried to follow those points in the months and years following. It worked.

CHAPTER SEVEN

My early training could not be complete without mentioning one of the most memorable events involving an inmate, "Ellsworth Raymond 'Bumpy' Johnson" (AZ 1117). Bumpy was an African-American who was known as the "Al Capone of Harlem." I was at Alcatraz for about 5 or 6 weeks and was sent with the training officer, Cecil "Red" Howell, to Oakland, California to meet a train and pick up several new prisoners. After picking up the prisoners we headed back to Alcatraz. I rode in the back with the six prisoners and Cecil drove the police patty wagon. Of course the inmates were fully chained and secured. Bumpy Johnson was one of these inmates and was a former prisoner of Alcatraz. Thus he was familiar with the prison, the rules and regulations and prison life. Bumpy had a rather bad reputation but he had a good sense of humor. During the trip he was telling the other inmates all about Alcatraz and scared the living daylight out of them. Later, after they were settled in Alcatraz, I was talking with Bumpy. He said, "You know boss, I think I left them other guys a little bit scared." I replied, "Me right along with them."

I realized that starting the next day I would begin the one month department training outlined in my one year training schedule. I looked forward to that. The shifts were normally month to month (day shift: 8 A.M. to 4 P.M.; night shift: 4 P.M. to midnight; and midnight shift: midnight to 8 A.M.).

Early in my tenure I realized having a "sixth sense" about inmates was critical to an officer's success. The ability to anticipate potential danger was critical and you always had to be on your toes because you were "enemy #1" in the eyes of inmates. Turn your back on the wrong inmate or situation and, the next thing you know, he's sticking you with a sharp object or breaking a rule. Also, I learned to be extremely careful, especially when it came to any type of personal relationship with an inmate. When performing my duties and responsibilities I tried to be "firm but fair"; no baloney stories, no lying to the inmates, follow-up on requests, and say "no" when appropriate. Relationships could easily be strained and stressful because even the slightest attempt to be nice or lenient (e.g., not taking action when warranted, looking the other way, etc.) could and probably would be seen as a weakness and the inmates could use that to their advantage. It was not to a guard's advantage to be easy on inmates, yet, a fine line had to be taken in order to gain respect and not be hated. I very quickly realized that there was no way in the world that I or any of the guards would know what the inmates were "really" up to or planning. All we could do was to stay alert at all times.

I did receive an excellent compliment from one of the inmates, Joseph Dayton Bright (AZ 1269). Joe worked in the Officer's mess. He told me that he watched me when I first started and stated, "that I was pretty cool and didn't fall for the inmate's sneaky ways of working a new guard to get advantages." This also confirmed to me that the early warnings I received were correct. Guards did not receive many compliments from inmates and when they did they were well received. I, on many occasions, wondered what inmates thought about me as I worked hard at treating them fairly, provided they followed the rules.

After finishing my daily on-the-job training and starting the monthly departmental training I had begun to feel a lot more comfortable with my surroundings. The early learning curve had been steep, but now I had found my groove. I watched as other trainees came and left. I was a survivor.

Veteran officers soon recognized I was not the typical "flash in the pan" and began to accept me as an insider. Job details were shared more openly and I learned facts about their families and personal lives. In the early days, they appeared reluctant to openly share believing I'd only be around for a few weeks. I was now somebody they could rely upon. I was part of "the club."

Even inmates seemed to accept me in their own kind of way. I survived the early "hazing" period where they challenged me and did their best to get into my head. I had heard it all…

"You're new…You don't know what's goin' on…"

"You're a fish! (always floundering around….)"

"How long are YOU gonna be here?!? The last guy made it a week before he quit!"

An inmates' philosophy, especially with rookies, seemed to be "you never know until you ask." They'd push as far as possible before being told "no."

"Mind if I have one of your smokes, Mr. Albright?"

"Wish I could have one of them Camels, this Bull Durham stuff is crap!"

"Got some gum for me?"

"Hey Mr. Albright, can you get me a cell change?"

"How "bout givin' me a good job recommendation?"

"Need a loan? I've got people outside here who can help ya!"

"My cousin has a construction business if you ever need any work done."

"When I get outta here, I'm gonna deliver a new tractor to your house…"

If a request violated prison rules, I'd simply re-state the regulation and my reason for disapproval. All inmates held a copy of prison rules in their cells and generally knew right from wrong. Once I established firm boundaries, life became a lot easier and extraneous requests were minimized.

Because I was young and physically fit, I was often asked to step in when physical force was required to subdue an inmate. In fact, I was included in a small group of young, tough officers given the unflattering title of "goon squad." I disliked this moniker because, in my opinion, a goon was someone who constantly bullied and brutalized people. I only used physical force when absolutely necessary to enforce rules and protect others. It was not my nature to intimidate or harass.

There were various repercussions when inmates broke prison rules. Officers were required to prepare a misconduct report (also known as a "shot") immediately after an infraction was committed. Penalties ultimately depended upon the seriousness of misconduct.

For lesser offenses, an inmate might only be verbally reprimanded or restricted from privileges (i.e., work, yard, visitors or movies). For more serious offenses (i.e., fighting, escape attempts, striking an officer, homosexual acts, etc.) an inmate would be sent to the Treatment Unit (segregation) in D-Block and/or lose "good time" credits. The only officials authorized to commit an inmate to segregation were the warden, associate warden, captain, or lieutenant.

The only "true" rights inmates had were shelter, food, medical and dental care and clothing. Everything else, including movies, library, visitors, recreation yard and mail, had to be earned. Officers held the right to withhold privileges if an inmate acted disrespectful or violated rules. I learned to "pick my spots" when withholding rights and only did so when it was absolutely necessary to get a point across.

I spent hours studying and learning the rules and always kept them nearby in case I had any questions. If a ruling fell into a "gray area" I would consult with a senior officer or my supervisor before making a final decision.

Running Alcatraz required tremendous teamwork. One hundred fifty employees served day and night, 365 days a year, to keep the

Rock solid. From the warden all the way down to an entry-level GS-5 correctional officer, everyone had a specific role assigned to them.

Tasks always had to be performed properly to avoid placing others at risk. For example, failure to catch a shiv (knife) at a snitch box (metal detector) might result in an officer or inmate getting stabbed. Improper shake down (searching) of a cell might result in an inmate O.D.'ing later that evening. An electrician's failure to properly repair lighting might contribute to a future escape attempt. No job detail could be over-looked. We relied upon each other like one large family.

Two executives were responsible for management of Alcatraz. The warden, Paul Madigan, was the chief official responsible for overall prison management and represented the U.S. Federal Bureau of Prisons. He was assisted by an Associate Warden, O.G. Blackwell, whose main responsibilities were safe and efficient prison operations including security of inmates.

Support personnel included people such as the superintendent of industries, business manager, assistant managers, records clerk, warden's secretary, captain's clerk, library attendant, plumbers, carpenters and electricians. All prison positions were filled by males as females were not offered employment inside prison grounds. Every employee had to be constantly alert and vigilant. Incarcerated inmates were constantly scheming and frequently developing imaginative and innovative escape scenarios. One of the shrewdest escape plans was thwarted by our Prison Record's Clerk, Joe Weaver. A released inmate forged a legal writ requiring a jailed Alcatraz inmate to appear in a San Francisco Court on a given date. Close scrutiny of the writ by Joe revealed an improper sequence of numbers on the court order. Quick follow-up with the court revealed the writ to be counterfeit. The ex-inmate was attempting to get his prison buddy into a position to initiate a possible escape while heading to court on the mainland.

Correctional officers represented the largest group of employees and included various ethnic groups. The officer force included 7 supervisors (1 captain and 6 lieutenants) and 89 non-supervisory correctional officers. Officers were classified as a GS-5 and GS-6 correctional officer, GS-7 senior officer and GS-8 senior officer specialist (position added in 1962). Positions such as control center officer, cellhouse west end officer (officer-in-charge) and clothing room officer were normally filled by senior officers. Most positions were filled by GS-5 and GS-6 junior officers.

Upon arriving at Alcatraz, I hired in as a GS-6 junior officer. This caused resentment amongst some tenured officers who still toiled as entry-level GS-5's. I understood their frustrations, but focused on keeping my head down and doing my job.

As I went through my training I kept copious notes in a little black book. Every position had its own detailed set of rules and routines. For example, kitchen duty not only required inmate supervision but also multiple utensil counts including items such as large knives and other sharp instruments. Specific procedures also had to be followed on food preparation and disposal. By taking notes I showed officers I was serious about learning their jobs. My black book also helped minimize repetitive job-related questions, therefore reducing the training officer's stress and workload. This was a small example of how I tried to work smart and gain the respect of those around me,

In the ongoing battle to stay one step ahead of inmates, I kept personal observations and notes about them in my black book. High-level thoughts included:

"Watch out for this guy, he'll strike an officer…"

"Murder, second degree…Doing 40 years and transferred from Leavenworth…"

"They nicknamed him 'The Lizard.' Ate a lizard while in San Quentin…"

I always strived to understand who inmates were and what made them tick. This information proved to be very useful, especially when handling confrontations. I generally knew their strengths, weaknesses and overall personality traits.

While I tried to learn to read inmates "like a book." I kept a more insular perspective in return. I never discussed my hobbies, family, political issues, sports, aches, pains, etc. In fact, it was considered "taboo" to get too close with inmates. Many inmates were professional cons who could turn around in a moment's notice and use personal information in their favor. Getting too close might even give an appearance of "favoritism" or worse yet, cloud your judgment when it came to matters of discipline.

It wasn't too long after I started the monthly departmental training sessions when the dock officer informed me that a one bedroom apartment would soon be available in the 64 Building. Getting Cathy and Kenny settled onto the island definitely helped lower my stress level. An Alcatraz guard's responsibilities were challenging enough let alone worrying about daily boat schedules and having family members located 5 miles away, including a 1.25 mile treacherous stretch of water. My daily commute would now consist of an easy 5 minute walk up and down a steep hill. I could even stop home for lunch and a kiss if I wanted to! I was anxious to discuss this with Cathy and make a decision.

United States Department of Justice
United States Penitentiary
Alcatraz, California

Date: August 5, 1959

Mr. James B. Albright
816 Nile
Aurora, Colorado

Dear Mr. Albright:

You have been selected for and are hereby offered a career-conditional appointment to the position of Correctional Officer, Grade GS-6, entrance salary $4490.00 a year, for duty at this institution. The appointment is subject to character investigation and retirement deduction, and a one year probationary period. Career-Conditional appointments become career appoints after three years of substantially continuous service. Appointees will supervise, safeguard, and train prisoners and carry out plans for correctional treatment. They will receive training in prison work, and those who do not complete the basic training satisfactorily will not be retained. Please refer to the examination announcement for full particulars concerning the position.

If you accept appointment you are requested to report at this institution at 9:00 A.M. on Monday, August 24, 1959 prepared to enter on duty. Please advise immediately if you will accept appointment and report at the time requested. This notification may be given by letter or telegram, or you may telephone our personnel office at Ordway 3-1437. If you will bring this letter with you, it will serve as a pass for you to board our prison launch leaving Dock #3, Fort Mason, situated at the foot of ~~Van Ness Avenue,~~ Laguna Street San Francisco, promptly at 8:20 A.M.

If you claimed 5-point veterans preference in the civil service examination for this position, please bring with you the original or photostatic copy of your military discharge certificate, which will be returned to you after inspection. If you are now employed by the Federal government and have annual leave which is transferrable under the leave regulations, such leave should be liquidated before you enter on duty at this institution. This may be accomplished by resigning your present Federal position after receiving this offer of appointment so that the period covered by the leave will expire before you enter on duty here. If you cannot liquidate your leave before the reporting date shown above, please inform us and consideration will be given to deferring the reporting date.

Enclosed you will find Standard Form 58 to bring your employment up to date, and Standard Form 86 Security Investigation Data. Please complete these forms and return them by mail to the institution as promptly as possible. Instructions for Form 86 are attached.

If you accept appointment I shall look forward to meeting you and having you become a member of our organization.

If you are single an effort will be made to take care of you in our bachelor quarters, but if you are married, it would be advisable to investigate the available housing in the San Francisco Bay Area before moving your family.

Sincerely,

P. J. MADIGAN
Warden

Jim's letter of acceptance for Federal Prison Service

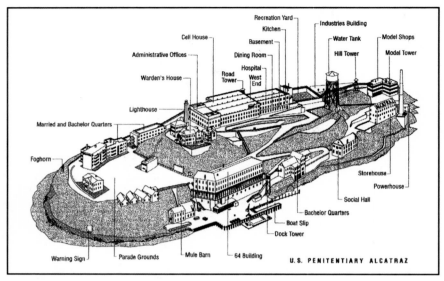

Diagram of Alcatraz Island

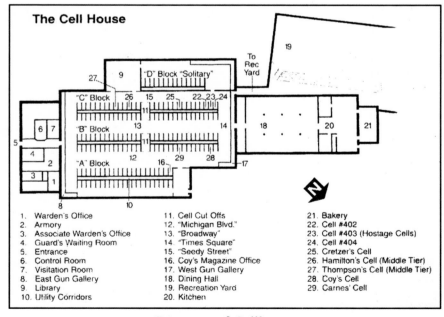

The Cell House

1. Warden's Office	11. Cell Cut Offs
2. Armory	12. "Michigan Blvd."
3. Associate Warden's Office	13. "Broadway"
4. Guard's Waiting Room	14. "Times Square"
5. Entrance	15. "Seedy Street"
6. Control Room	16. Coy's Magazine Office
7. Visitation Room	17. West Gun Gallery
8. East Gun Gallery	18. Dining Hall
9. Library	19. Recreation Yard
10. Utility Corridors	20. Kitchen

21. Bakery
22. Cell #402
23. Cell #403 (Hostage Cells)
24. Cell #404
25. Cretzer's Cell
26. Hamilton's Cell (Middle Tier)
27. Thompson's Cell (Middle Tier)
28. Coy's Cell
29. Carnes' Cell

Diagram of Cellhouse

BOAT SCHEDULE

Leaving Ft. Mason

Weekly	Saturday	Sunday	Holiday
A.M.	A.M.	A.M.	A.M.
12:25	12:25	12:25	12:25
6:55	7:20	7:20	7:20
7:35	8:25	8:25	8:25
8:25	9:15	9:15	9:15
10:15	10:15	10:15	10:15
	11:15	11:15	11:15
P.M.	P.M.	P.M.	P.M.
1:00	1:00	1:00	1:00
3:35	3:35	3:35	3:35
4:10			
4:55	5:10	5:10	5:10
5:25			
5:55	5:55	5:55	5:55
7:15	7:15	7:15	7:15
9:00	9:00	9:00	9:00
10:15	10:15	10:15	10:15
11:30	11:30	11:30	11:30

(Reverse Side Leaving Alcatraz)

Boat Schedule

BOAT SCHEDULE

Leaving Alcatraz

Weekly	Saturday	Sunday	Holiday
A.M.	A.M.	A.M.	A.M.
12:10	12:10	12:10	12:10
6:40	7:05	7:05	7:05
7:20	8:10	8:10	8:10
8:10	9:00	9:00	9:00
10:00	10:00	10:00	10:00
	11:00	11:00	11:00
P.M.	P.M.	P.M.	P.M.
12:45	12:45	12:45	12:45
3:20	3:20	3:20	3:20
3:55	4:55	4:55	4:55
4:40	5:40	5:40	5:40
5:10	7:00	7:00	7:00
5:40	8:45	8:45	8:45
7:00	10:00	10:00	10:00
8:45	11:15	11:15	11:15
10:00			
11:15			

(Reverse Side Leaving Ft. Mason)

Boat Schedule

Jim's prison ID issued 8-24-59

Aerial photo of lighthouse, Wardens, Doctor's houses & Adm.
bldg., cellhouse & A bldg.

Sign on East beach warning people to stay off Island.

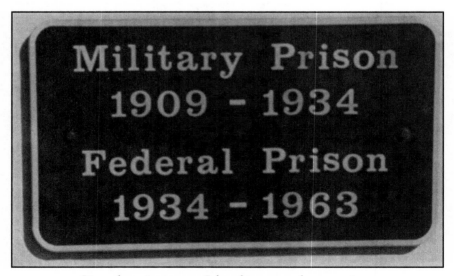

Military Prison
1909 - 1934
Federal Prison
1934 - 1963

Sign showing years Island was used as a prison

Jim in New Control Center 1962

Warden Johnson used to ferry residents to and from the Island

Tower #1 Dock Tower

Menu of last meal served on Island

Jim and Cathy on refurbished Alcatraz firetruck. Jim was a
member of the fire crew while there

Stairs to nowhere in 64 bldg, across hall from apartment

Cathy looking out bedroom window of apt. 302. Curtains she made are still hanging in bedroom.

CHAPTER EIGHT

As much as we enjoyed the city, our patience and pocket book grew thin while waiting for an island apartment. Being informed that one was available was extremely pleasing to both Cathy and I and we were excited and anxious to move. Our ideal preference would have been a 2-bedroom unit in the newer A-B-C apartments on the west side of the Parade Ground, but we quickly decided to take anything we could get.

On October 12, 1959, we made what was to be our final rent payment in the city of San Francisco. We bought a three room group of furniture to be delivered to the Fort Mason dock which would then be shipped to Alcatraz for our apartment. We hurried to Fort Mason to eagerly await the arrival of the prison boat. We had nothing more than a few pieces of luggage with us to take across to the island. Cathy's cedar chest and our furniture would arrive later via the barge.

Upon arriving at the Fort Mason dock parking lot we were pleasantly surprised when several "Islanders" volunteered to unload our belongings. We learned this neighborly assistance reflected a long standing tradition. All my co-workers and their spouses regularly pitched in to help with groceries, packages, luggage and any other items that would travel across on the boat. The Boat ran a strict schedule and waited for no one. We found little use for an automobile for the next several years and were very thankful for the "perk" of free parking. The last thing I did before locking our car was to hide a pistol recently purchased in San Francisco. This weapon partially guaranteed our security while traveling and shopping in the City.

Normally, Cathy would have been very nervous about traveling across a large body of water in a small boat. She had never been fond of boats and usually declined boating invitations on inland lakes. Her nervousness was soon tempered, however, by the excitement of finally "coming home" to our own apartment on Alcatraz. Kenny was grinning from ear-to-ear as the Warden Johnston bobbed across the waves. Much to the amusement of other passengers he ran from side-to-side trying to look out the windows. This would be the first of many trips in the next 4 years for Cathy and Kenny.

We were welcomed island-side by dock personnel and received help unloading from the same people that assisted us at Fort Mason. Our belongings were immediately loaded into the back of the island truck which was often used for hauling large loads coming off the boat. We thanked everyone and the three of us walked up to our new home, apartment number 64-108. The truck drove around behind the apartment to meet us.

In order to gain access to our apartment, it was necessary to climb the stairs near the base of the dock tower and take the walkway to the first floor of 64 Building. The truck pulled up to the stairway, which led down to our apartment, and the driver helped me carry the few bags down the stairs. Before entering our apartment, Cathy and Kenny looked up in amazement at the warden's and doctor's residence seemingly teetering on the cliffs 75 feet overhead. I then summoned them to follow me down the stairs to see their new digs.

I unlocked the door to apartment 108 with a key obtained the previous day from the Warden's secretary. As the peeling old door squeaked open and daylight appeared in the small kitchen, I immediately noticed several small black bugs scurrying for cover. Cockroaches were a perpetual problem in 64 Building because flour, sugar and other food items were stored in the basement just below the apartments. Even though many people in the building sprayed their apartments regularly, the bugs still ruled the roost.

Luckily, Cathy hadn't spotted the cockroaches and happily brought Kenny in just behind me. After all, I didn't want to spoil her first day in the Taj Mahal! We walked around the small apartment that basically consisted of one bedroom and two 9X12 rooms. Kenny toddled along with us and we showed him the perfect place for his new bedroom – the dining room of course! Being a two-year-old, he didn't seem to care and was more concerned about checking out his new stomping grounds. We opened the door off the living room, which led to the balcony, and took in the beautiful view of the East Bay. Below us, the Warden Johnston was still sitting at the dock waiting to carry its next load of passengers to the mainland. A friendly dockworker spotted us, waved, and yelled up asking how we liked our new apartment. "Uh, great.", I half-heartedly replied thinking of the bugs I had to exterminate. "Great view!", Cathy cheerfully added. "GGweeat!", mimicked Kenny.

After getting our bags situated in the only bedroom, my next task was to notify the downstairs dock office to transport our recently purchased furniture up to the apartment. It arrived shortly thereafter.

As luck would have it, a thick fog rolled in our first evening in the apartment and the foghorns on both ends of the island began sounding at 30-second intervals all night long. I slept like a baby that night, but Cathy and Kenny couldn't sleep a wink. She thought the foghorn sound was just "awful" and wondered whether she'd ever get used to the mournful drone. Eventually, she learned to live with the racket.

Our initial monthly rent was only $27.50, roughly one-third the cost of our San Francisco apartment, and was deducted directly from my paycheck. Rent included all utilities and even included laundry and dry cleaning at the prison laundry facilities. Other island apartments rented for as much as $35.00 per month, but those were generally 2 bedrooms and were located in the newer B and C Buildings.

If Cathy had any fears about moving to the Rock and being near hardened criminals, she certainly never voiced them. I often talked about how Alcatraz civilians were probably safer than the average San Francisco civilian due to the high security. Several prisoners worked the dock area just below our apartment, but they were under constant surveillance by the dock tower guards and ground personnel. In fact, many of our neighbors felt safe enough to never even lock their doors!

Living on Alcatraz took some adjustment. Basic food staples, fruit, vegetables, and meat could be purchased in the island store located on the first floor of 64 Building. For a wider selection and variety of food, you planned your shopping trip according to the boat schedule. A Safeway was conveniently located near Fort Mason. In fact, our life basically revolved around the boat schedule when going back and forth to the mainland for recreation, shopping and, in later years, Kenny's schooling.

A small post office was located next door to the store in the 64 Building. This was one of the oldest operating U.S. Post Office branches in the San Francisco region having been established during the military period in 1876. Our postmistress, Billie-Jean Long, was appointed in 1957 and was responsible for sorting incoming mail and shipping outgoing pre-censored inmate correspondence. A Pelican postal mark was stamped on all outgoing mail. The name "Alcatraz" was derived from the Spanish reference to the island of "Alcatraces" or Pelicans. Later I learned it was also defined as "strange bird." Kenny would often go down to the post office to fetch mail and was often told by Billie-Jean that there was "no mail". Pretty soon, Kenny began referring to her as "No Mail" because he had heard those words so many times.

Alcatraz's electricity was generated in the island's power plant and was the antiquated direct current variety (as opposed to the more modern alternating current). Appliances were not normally manufactured to handle direct current and needed a DC converter to operate properly. We bought a converter from island residents. Water was brought in by barge twice weekly and pumped into the water tower.

We spent the first nights on our balcony admiring the well-lit Bay Bridge and the lights over in the East Bay. We went up to the Parade Grounds one night at sunset, and were treated to a spectacular view of the Golden Gate Bridge and the City of San Francisco at dusk. Even the least romantic person would find it hard not to be affected under the influence of these views at night.

Early mornings were often special on the east end of the island. The hours between 5 A.M. and 7 A.M. were generally very quiet as the prevailing winds were calm and very few people were milling around the dock area. I initially worked the early shift in the dock tower and was treated to some spectacular sunrises. The sun would leave a long trail across the bay and the white face of the 64 Building seemed to change colors as the sun rose in the sky. George Black, a fellow officer, would often stand on his balcony, coffee cup in hand as the sun rose and would watch his kids leave for school on the 7 am boat.

Temperatures were generally temperate on the dock side of the island because it was protected from the westerly breezes. Temperatures were a lot cooler on the opposite west end of the island because there was nothing there to block the wind. You could be in shirtsleeves at the dock end and on the same day require a full coat to be comfortable on the west side. In general, temperatures were in the 60's year-round and rarely deviated more than 10 degrees. It only snowed once during our 4 years on the island.

If the frequent sound of the foghorns weren't enough, dockside residents of 64 Building were treated every week to 24 straight hours of two roaring diesel engines that pumped water from a barge. Unfortunately, the barge parked right outside the building and pumped water into a nearby pipe that ran up the hill to the water tower. The island's water requirements were significant. 1.5 million gallons of fresh water per month (50,000 gallons per day) were required to sustain overall operations. In addition, 33,000 gallons of seawater were also used per day for flushing toilets in the cellhouse. Cathy was "thrilled" the first time she experienced the chorus of diesels and foghorns in unison. This "beautiful music" was further enhanced by barking seals and squawking seagulls. Cathy quickly grew accustomed to this cacophony of sound and tuned out the most irritating noises.

Kenny and I enjoyed watching the boats that frequently motored by the island. The favorites were the large overseas container ships coming and going with imported goods. Most impressive were the large Navy vessels. We remembered the aircraft carriers, in particular, the USS Enterprise. It was spectacular to see the sailors standing shoulder-to-shoulder at attention on the flight deck in dress whites and the fire boats saluting them with sprays of water. All of this show with the skyline of San Francisco in the background. Also, the submarines did the same thing. These ships were headed for the Navy Yard in Oakland. Tour and party boats were always circling the island giving hungry tourists a glimpse of the ROCK and having fun. On quieter days, you could almost hear every amusing word over the tour boat loudspeakers talking about the hard life on the Rock and the incorrigible living up in the cellhouse. I knew if we could hear the sounds of people having fun so could the inmates. Sailboats often filled the bay on the weekends and frequently you could hear the sound of their sails popping as they came about.

Our first Thanksgiving on Alcatraz was a quiet but thankful occasion. By Christmas time, we had been befriended by several island families and shared in numerous formal and informal holiday events. We missed our family and friends back in Iowa and Colorado, but our new island "family" certainly made the holidays brighter.

After 4 months into our tour on Alcatraz, we decided to throw out the one-year probation countdown clock and focus on the wonders of our new island home. 1959 had come in like a lion, but was heading out like a lamb. Life on the Rock wasn't so hard after all!

CHAPTER NINE

I enthusiastically looked forward to the day when my training would be over and I would be "on my own." When that day finally arrived I was excited, and for the first time thought of myself as an experienced, seasoned guard. The valuable and extensive training, experiences and interaction with the other guards and officers, coupled with the learning process of guarding, monitoring and controlling the inmates, gave me confidence that I was ready. I really started to feel at ease.

I cannot emphasize enough the electric feeling that went through my veins whenever I entered the main cellhouse through the gate and heard the "ringing noise" of the closing of the metal door. It was awesome. This was by far one of the most exciting events in my entire career with the Federal Prison Service.

The posts and shifts were changed monthly in the first year of employment, and quarterly after the training was completed. At one time or another I worked every post - from junior officer in a tower to Acting Lieutenant of the watch.

Numerous supervisory personnel and guards were on duty in the main cellhouse. I remembered thinking, here I am, with 260 notorious inmates, most of whom were to varying degrees some of the most uncontrollable inmates in any prison, and I now felt that I knew them and thought by now they know me; however, how much did we really know each other? I recalled the "finger" gesture when I first walked through on my introductory tour and thought "What are these well behaved individuals up to? What would I really see and find? What lies ahead?" Sometimes, in a way, I felt like a prisoner myself, locked in and no place to go. I thought about some of the horror stories that I was told, read about, or saw in the movies, and this added to my apprehension. I had only to rely on the training and experiences I obtained at Alcatraz.

It was interesting that shortly after I started at Alcatraz I had the opportunity, along with five other guards, to visit the California State Prison at San Quentin. The prison held approximately 5,000 inmates assigned 5 or 6 to a cell – versus the 260 inmates at Alcatraz each confined to an individual cell. During our return to Alcatraz I remember telling the other guards "What a difference, I don't think I would like those arrangements."

The main cellhouse at Alcatraz was probably the most difficult area overall to supervise, guard and patrol. It was the inmate's home away from home. The layout of the cells that housed the inmates and the other facilities contained within the main cellhouse were well designed to not only control orderly movement of the inmates, but to also monitor their activities.. There were four cell blocks (A, B, C and D), a kitchen, dining room, bakery, library, barber shop, hospital, clothing room, shower area, band room and movie/chapel room. Approximately 75% of an inmate's time was spent in one fashion or another in these areas.

When entering the main cellhouse the four cell blocks were the first thing I saw. There was a deadly silence and an ominous welcome to the world of the inmates. I began to think that my earlier confidence, about being on my own, might have been a bit premature. Even though I had entered this area many times before it still left me with an uncomfortable feeling, one of uncertainty and trepidation. This feeling would sometimes change throughout the day and night as activities occurred. What also caught my attention was that all the cell blocks contained 3 tiers of cells and that the 3rd tier of each block did not reach the ceiling, but the metal bars did. There was a large space between the top of the 3rd tier and the ceiling. Further, none of the cell blocks adjoined with any outside wall. They were in the middle of a large room.

Cell Block-A contained 124 cells, one side faced north toward the outside wall of the prison, the other side faced inward toward B-Block. A-Block was the oldest of the blocks and dated back to the military prison in the early 1900s. While I was there it did not house inmates but, was mainly used for storage. The cells were never modernized and the bars were of the old soft flat iron materials, not the more modern rounded, hard-steel bars of the other three cell blocks.

The general inmate population was only housed in Cell Blocks B and C. Each cell block contained 168 cells – each cell being 5 feet wide, 9 feet deep and 7 feet high. A sliding grille door, controlled by a locking device at the end of each cell block, allowed the guards to lock and open the cell doors to let the inmates in and out.

The cells of B and C Block were never filled to capacity as regulations limited the number of inmates that could be assigned to the prison. Two cells located at the west end of C-Block were not filled, but were used for bathrooms by the guards and as a space to perform strip searches of the inmates. I was able to get the uncomfortable feeling of what it felt like to go to the bathroom without any privacy. The top two tiers were most favored by the inmates because of the view. The centralized cell locking system, with levers, allowed the guards to open or close all cells in a range, or just a number of cells at a time, or individually.

Cell Blocks B and C were split in two with a passage, called "cutoffs" or "crossways." They were midway between each of the cell blocks, thus allowing guards to quickly pass between them. When I first entered these cutoffs, looking up around the fire extinguisher hose on the wall, I could see the bullet holes that remained from the shooting that took place in one of the much earlier escape attempts.

I could also see where the Army had chopped a hole in the roof to drop hand grenades into the cell blocks from the 1946 riots.

All cell Blocks had narrow utility corridors which were large enough to walk into. They contained the plumbing, electricity, ventilation, etc., for the cells. Since Cell Block D only had one side, the corridor was inward facing Cell Block C. A door at the end of each tier of the cell blocks allowed entry into these utility corridors.

One night at about 5:30 P.M., at the end of my shift, I was about to leave and go home, when I heard water running in the plumbing corridor of B-Block. I assumed it was a broken pipe. Another guard, Charles Hermann, was also leaving. I said, "You get the key to let me in, I'll go and shut the water off." Officer Hermann went, got the key and opened the corridor entry door for me to enter. It was very dark. On the top of the 3rd tier there was a 2" X 10" board that was used as a means to walk across, as there was no floor above the initial entrance to the corridor. I started across the board, 15 feet or so and saw the water spraying across the board, so I decided not to walk across but to crawl up on top of the cell block and shut the water off. After turning the water off I returned to the main floor and Officer Hermann and I went on home, thinking nothing about it, just a broken pipe. I remember telling Officer Hermann "It is really dark up there with those damn blankets hanging and they shouldn't be there." The top of the cell block was being cleaned and painted and the blankets were allowed to be hung so as to not let dust or paint fall on the main floors. Later in the book this will be thoroughly discussed in the Anglin/Morris escape. The next day the plumber fixed the pipe. I have no idea how the pipe got broken and really didn't think much about it. After the escape, I remembered the incident and realized that there was a strong probability that one of the escapees had crawled up to the top of the cell block where they were working on their escape route – inside the "protection" of those damn blankets, and broke the water pipe. One or possibly two of them probably were up there, but hiding, while I was shutting off the water. If that was the case, luck was with me, for had I discovered them or they discovered me, it could have proven fatal, especially to me.

The openings that surrounded the cell blocks all had their own names. I was told that the names were given by the inmates. "Times Square" was the name for the cross at the west end of the cell blocks and the other openings, between the cell blocks, ran into Times Square. Most all routes from the cells – hospital, dining, clothing, exercise yard, etc – went through Time Square. "Broadway" was the opening between B and C Blocks; Michigan Avenue between A and B Blocks which got its name from inmates from Michigan, and "Seedy" Avenue between C and D Blocks which got its name because it was between C and D block. They often razzed inmates on the other side because they didn't have "Seedy" Avenue's view.

Officer Gene "Tweety" Glaum, an Air Force Pilot during the war, was an excellent guard with a good sense of humor and well respected by both the inmates and guards. He loved the San Francisco Giants baseball team. The inmates knew of his passion for the Giants and would tease him, especially when they were losing. When he was leaving to go home and would be walking down Broadway, many of the inmates, from their cells, would say something to him about the Giants, such as: "Mr. Glaum, What's the matter with those Giants? What is going on?" Officer Glaum would respond "Don't go away I'll be right back." The inmates liked him and as such he could get away with joking.

In each cell, except for the cells in D-Block, light fixtures were positioned on the ceiling and could be controlled by both the inmate and the guard; however, all lights were out at 9:30 P.M.

D-Block was the last and most interesting of the Cell Blocks because it made up the Discipline/Treatment Unit – referred to as segregation or the hole. This cell block was a world in itself. It was for punishment and separation from the main population. The cells of D-Block only faced the south wall of the prison. There were 42 cells (36 segregation and 6 Dark Hole cells). The cells were larger than cells in the other cell blocks as they were never converted to the smaller sizes. Cells 1-8 on tier 1 were 3 feet deeper than the cells above them on tiers 2 and 3. Some of the cell doors in D-Block were operated electronically by the cellhouse officer and the West Gun Gallery guard working together.

Lights in D-Block, except the dark hole, were very bright and remained on continuously. This made it very difficult to sleep and inmates would be up half the night, some all night, and they would sleep during the day. Some would read continuously and sleep when they could.

The south wall of the prison had barred windows and the inmates on the second and third tiers could see the Marina at Fort Mason and other sights of San Francisco through the front of their cells. This was ironic as it was the Treatment Unit (punishment) and yet it had the best view in the house.

Typically, inmates who broke the rules, gave guards a bunch of guff, or were disagreeable, uncontrollable or unstable to the point that they had to be kept apart from the other inmates, would be temporarily assigned to one of these punishment cells for a little "attitude" adjustment.

Inmates in segregation were allowed one shower per week. A cell located at the end of D-Block contained a small vestibule with a sink and shower and was where these inmates took their showers. They were not allowed to go to the shower room. Also, they were allowed one hour per week in the exercise yard, but not with the general population.

There was no limit to the amount of time an inmate could be assigned to segregation; however, most were for 30 days or less. As was mentioned earlier, Robert Stroud, The Birdman, was one extreme example of an inmate who was assigned to segregation for years.

If an inmate was assigned to segregation for an extended period of time, all his personal effects would be packed and removed from his cell in the general population; however, if approved by the Warden, he was allowed to have some of his personal effects. When he returned to the general population he would normally be assigned a different or less desirable cell than the one he initially occupied. This was also done as a form of punishment as other inmates who followed rules and regulation could be assigned to a more coveted cell.

When an inmate was sent to segregation he was issued only a pair of coveralls. The guard in segregation would call the guard in the clothing room and a pair would be delivered to the segregation officer. Before issuing the coveralls to the inmate, a thorough shakedown was conducted, including collars, seams, etc. Inmates would attempt to hide cigarette papers, razor blades, tobacco, matches, or whatever in various parts of the coveralls. On one occasion I recall razor blades being found in the seams. When I first arrived, inmates in segregation were not allowed cigarettes or tobacco; however, Bull Durham tobacco was allowed later as the rules were loosened.

Blankets and mattresses were provided to the inmates daily and were stored in Cell 8 of D-Block. Inmates who were put in segregation were subject to strict controls including two daily thorough shakedowns; one at 3:30 P.M., when a blanket and mattress would be issued and another at 9:00 A.M., when the blanket and mattress would be taken back. These shakedowns included a strip search of the inmates, both the coveralls they wore and their body parts, and a thorough search of the mattress and blankets they turned in and were issued.

Inmates in segregation would receive meals in their cells and was normally a reduced amount. They ate a little earlier than the rest of the population as time was needed for the kitchen crew to prepare the food and the delivery to segregation by inmate orderlies. Before the food was sent to segregation from the kitchen, the Lieutenant would inspect the food and say "they don't need this or that food item" and would take something off the tray. Then when it arrived at D-Block the segregation officer would do the same. It might be something the inmate liked.

I recall one instance when an inmate acted up on purpose to get put in segregation so he could lose weight. Inmates who were in segregation were put on a dietary program, restricted calories and certain types of food. He told me that he did this as a means of a forced diet, and it worked. He stated "I know I needed your help and without it I wouldn't have made it." He was in isolation for 28 days and lost 25 pounds.

If an inmate observed the rules in segregation (excluding those in the DARK HOLE) they could go out to the recreation yard for only one hour per week on weekdays. The general prison population had their opportunity to go to the recreation yard only on weekends.

Inmates acted up even in segregation. I remember an incident involving Homer Clinton (AZ 1294), also known as the "Green Lizard" because I understand he once ate a lizard. When I was patrolling the segregation cell block, he was standing at the bars of his cell and the rest of the inmates in D-Block were hollering and raising hell, trying to stir up trouble. We called this a "Shit Storm." As I approached his cell I saw Homer had a religious picture on a piece of yarn around his neck which he wore like a necklace. I asked him "Lizard, what do you have around your neck?" He laughed and told me that it was a picture of someone in his family. I said something about him not having relatives or words to that affect and he thought that was very funny. He burst out laughing and then started joking about it. He got some of the other inmates laughing which in turn quieted things down.

Occasionally, an inmate in D-Block wouldn't shave or get his hair cut, which they were required to do. On one occasion when I was in the gun gallery, the segregation guard yelled up for me to open one of the cells. The guard took the inmate up to the front of D-Block to get a hair cut and shower. The inmate refused. He was then held down and given both a haircut and shower.

The strictest punishment at Alcatraz during my four years was being assigned to one of the six cells – 9 through 14- in D-Block, called the DARK HOLE. An inmate would be assigned to one of these dreaded cells when more severe attitude adjustments were needed, or when an extremely serious rule violation occurred. Being placed in a dark hole cell meant solitary confinement and isolation. These cells were called the Dark Hole cells because being confined to one meant you would be in complete darkness at all times. There were no lights in the cells and a solid steel door blocked out any outside light. Before entering the actual "dark hole" cell, the guard would open the locked solid steel door which opened into a 3 foot vestibule. Once inside the vestibule, the inmate would enter the actual cell through a sliding barred door. Then the inmate was locked in the cell and the guard would exit through the solid steel door and lock it thus making the area inside the cell totally dark. There was a small opening on the solid steel door which only the guard could open and close to briefly observe the inmate.

To make things even worse for an inmate assigned to a Dark Hole Cell, three of the six dark hole cells contained a toilet and sink whereas the other three contained nothing and were called "bare" cells. These three bare cells only had a simple hole in the steel floor which served for a toilet. Inmates, for extreme rule violations or serious misconduct, etc., would be placed naked in one of these three bare cells. Also, inmates assigned to any of the Dark Hole cells were not issued a blanket or mattress.

The maximum time an inmate would be assigned to a dark hole cell was for 30 days; however, most would be for less than 3 days. An inmate could be let out of the dark hole and within several days be returned, if appropriate.

One of the most interesting things to the three dark hole cells that had toilets was that they could only be flushed by a guard from the back of the cell – from the utility corridor. Occasionally, if an inmate acted up or was creating a problem, the guard, including myself, would not flush the toilet and when the inmate would make a comment about it not being flushed or needing to be flushed, I would tell him "we are going to do it but I am busy right now."

CHAPTER TEN

Few inmates were assigned directly to Alcatraz but were transferred from other prisons. When they arrived at Alcatraz they found the discipline more rigorous and structured than at any prison they had been accustomed to in the past. The reason they were normally transferred from other prisons was because they either refused to conform to the rules and regulations at the other Federal Prison, resisted authority, were extremely violent, or were considered escape risks. Their conduct was such that it was detrimental to the institutions as well as the institution's inmates. They were some of the most dangerous and they earned their way in by their bad conduct; however, they could likewise earn their way out by being good. If Alcatraz prison officials felt an inmate no longer posed a threat and could follow rules and regulations, the inmate could then be transferred to another Federal Institution to finish his sentence. Being assigned to Alcatraz was by no means a permanent assignment. These inmates were accorded the same rights to apply for parole, etc., as any other inmate at other federal institutions, and they did.

However, Alcatraz was much stricter than other institutions and certain privileges allowed at other institutions were not afforded at Alcatraz. It was a maximum security penitentiary, with an aura of mystery surrounding it and a reputation of being escape proof.

Statistics, reflecting a breakdown of offenses committed by the 264 inmates who were in Alcatraz on June 30, 1959, a few months prior to my arrival, were as follows:

Bank Robbery	92
Murder	34
Housebreaking, Robbery, Assault	26
N.M.V.T.A. (car theft)	24
Kidnapping	22
Narcotics	17
Violations Postal Laws	8
Rape	8
Assault to Murder	6
Counterfeit	5
Transporting Firearms Interstate	5
Assault, Mutiny, Riot	4
Other charges	13
Total	264
Life Sentence	24
Total time in years and months	5,441 years & 6 months
Average sentence – excluding Life	20.6 years
Average age of Inmates	35 ½

The prison normally held, on average, about 260 inmates and the following numbers by day, month and year reflect the inmates on Alcatraz at that particular time: June 30, 1959 – 264; August 31, 1960 – 251; July 31, 1961 – 249; August 31, 1962 – 260; November 30, 1961 – 232; and March 21, 1963 – 0. Warden Blackwell felt the "ideal" count was between 275 and 280. This he felt would benefit manning the industrial shops. Frank Lucas Bolt (AZ 1) was the first inmate and Frank Clay Weatherman (AZ 1576) was the last inmate admitted. Several inmates returned more than once; however, they did not retain their old number but were reissued a new inmate number. An example of this is James "Blackie" Audett who was in Alcatraz on 3 separate occasions, and his inmate numbers were AZ 208, AZ 551 and AZ 1217.

Black and white inmates were segregated by design in several areas of the prison. The cellhouse was one area where black and white inmates were segregated. Black inmates were assigned cells on the inside of B-Block facing C-Block. Black inmates were assigned to all three tiers on inside B-Block. Black kitchen workers were assigned to the bottom tier on the west end closest to the kitchen and dining room entrance.

The dining room and shower room were the only other area where black and white inmates were segregated. Since inmates entering these areas entered by tier, and since black inmates were all in one tier, they all entered at the same time. Also, within the dining room specific tables were arranged that were designated specifically for black inmates. In all other areas; such as the industries, movies, and recreation yard, black and white inmates mingled and played together. Each inmate was treated the same.

There were fewer privileges, tighter security, and the island had a psychological effect on the inmates from its "tough and forbidding" prison reputation. For some, the strict discipline and controls was a positive. The stricter surveillance and discipline gave the inmate a certain feeling of protection; however, that was not always the case. Each inmate created his own unique set of problems. Some abused privileges, were disruptive, did not conform, did not follow the rules, etc.

An inmate's life in Alcatraz really started before entering a cell. When Alcatraz was notified that a prisoner was assigned to them, the date and time of his arrival, etc., the prisoner would be met in San Francisco or Oakland and escorted to Alcatraz by way of Pier 4 at Fort Mason on the boat Warden Johntson. They were handcuffed, belly chained and had leg irons before boarding and would be escorted. Since there was only one boat, they were transported along with other visitors and people going or returning to the island. The inmates were put in a different area of the boat (usually the bow) and kept away from the other passengers. Just imagine the feeling a prisoner must have felt getting ready to board the boat for Alcatraz and during the journey over. He can see the "ROCK" and he must have know it's reputation, real or perceived, and there he is chained and shackled in a cold boat.

When the boat arrived at the dock at Alcatraz, the inmates would get off last. They went through a metal detector, got on the bus, and were transported up to the clothing room. If there was only one new inmate they would normally take him through the front door, down Broadway to the clothing room. If there was several, they would take them directly through the basement to the clothing room. When the inmate arrived in the clothing room they would be met by the Medical Technician Associate (MTA). Here the inmates would strip, be strip searched (look everywhere including mouth, in the nose, in the anus, between the toes, etc.) to ensure they had nothing. They would then take a shower and be given prison clothing, be assigned to a cell and given a prison number (the number assigned would be the next number in numerical order from the last number assigned and that number would never be assigned to another prisoner nor would it be reissued if a prisoner left and later returned), and taken to the cell. In a couple of days the inmate would be classified as to what level he would be and where he would work. Usually they liked to start new inmates in the kitchen.

The reputation of a prisoner's life on Alcatraz was that it was harsh and cruel; however this was not totally correct. It was rigorous, highly disciplined and not easy; however, the conditions weren't really that more difficult than at any Federal Penitentiary. Privileges were more tightly controlled and living was different. The food was good and if prisoners adhered to the rules their privileges were good. Three squares, clothing, and medical attention were the only things guaranteed a prisoner; everything else was a privilege that the inmate had to earn. Privileges were earned and only those inmates who deserved them got them. They could and were easily withheld for violations of rules, misconduct, or in some cases just to get a point across. It quickly became apparent to the inmates that the facility was deteriorating, expensive to maintain, and that more and more procedures and policies were being relaxed. The fact that these were the most notorious, violent and hardened criminals had to be kept in mind at all times with the realization that many inmates constantly looked for any opportunities, to get an edge.

A prisoner's daily routine was strictly controlled and highly regimented and there was little variation from day to day. It became more lenient in the four years I was there especially with the change in wardens. There were many idle hours and boredom was probably the number one concern for prisoners. In order to stimulate an inmate and help him fight boredom, numerous strictly controlled activities and facilities, all of which were privileges that had to be earned and could easily be withheld, were made available. This included working, reading, movies, music, radio, art, library, the recreation yard, etc. There was no television, very few educational programs, no privacy with even the porcelain toilets being visible from the cell door. There were no windows except that inmates on the 2nd and 3rd tier of D-Block could look out through the front of their cells and through the windows of the South side of the prison wall and see San Francisco. The inmates lived in cell blocks with small cells. Inmates, other than the kitchen orderlies who worked seven days a week, worked five days each week. Each inmate was issued a booklet called "Institution Rules & Regulations" and they were required to keep it in their cell at all times. These rules and regulations listed everything including daily routines, counts, general rules, clothing, medical attention, yard privileges, work regulations, etc. I have a copy of the Institution Rules & Regulations – Inmate Reg. Number, 1226. For example that booklet lists the daily routine as starting 7:00 A.M. on weekdays and 7:15 A.M. on weekends. It also contains the number of counts to be taken and the time of each count. For example: 5:30 P.M. was listed as final lock-up count for weekdays and 4:40 for Saturdays, Sundays and Holidays.

Many of the inmates assigned to Alcatraz were difficult to deal with and brought with them experience and prison smarts. They became experts in deceiving those around them. They were adept at listening and taking mental notes of information. They knew every guard, their habits, strengths and weaknesses, and what that guard would do before he did it. There was no real behavioral treatment program at Alcatraz and few inmates changed. Prisoners were very creative and would, on occasions try to "GET EVEN WITH THE GUARDS." Their methods varied and rarely were they physical; however, they had other methods such as mental abuse, showing contempt for authority, and just being stubborn and negative. They would argue, make smart remarks, insult, spit, or if a guard lied to them, urine or feces may be thrown at them. There were always the obscene gestures such as lifting the middle finger. Occasionally an inmate would physically strike a guard. They would attempt to make a guard's life miserable and difficult. For these type deeds, inmates would forfeit good time already earned, lose privileges, or be sent to the Treatment Unit (D-Block) segregation.

Occasionally an inmate would burn a mattress or blow up his toilet. The inmate would use a cup to empty the water from his toilet, and then pour the water in his sink. Rags or paper would be used to dry the toilet, getting it good and dry. Paper or clothing or whatever would burn would be put in the toilet and set on fire. After letting it get good and hot, the plunger would be pulled and when the cold water hit the fire it would blow the porcelain toilet into a thousand pieces. Before the inmate pulled the plunger he would put his mattress up in front of him for protection. Pieces of the toilet and mattress would go clear out of his cell into the walkways. He would do this to raise hell. The inmate also knew he was going to segregation and would have to clean-up his cell and the mess he made. The next day the inmate plumber plus the civilian mechanic/plumber would put in a new toilet. This didn't happen very often. Most inmates just wanted to do their time and be left alone.

The inmates had their own "code of silence" and would not tell on each other. Procedures required that whenever anything occurred every inmate who was in the area was questioned. Normally this produced nothing as the inmates would say they "saw or heard nothing." If the situation went to court at a later date this statement could be used against the inmates.

Inmates did not have positive feelings for other inmates who were child molesters, as many had children of their own. These inmates had to walk a thin line.

Inmates had few rights other than legal actions through the legal system. There was a process called PMB (Prison Mail Box) where an inmate could write to any official they wanted. This mail was not censored and was sent sealed. I assume the official receiving the PMB would, if appropriate, call the warden and inform him that he received a PMB from a particular inmate and would discuss it with the warden. This procedure was in force the whole time I was there. Additionally, the Warden would occasionally walk around and the inmates could ask him questions or talk with him. On rare occasions when the Director of the Bureau of Prisons would visit and walk around the inmates could also ask him questions and talk to him.

If an inmate had a complaint against a guard he had several methods to use to register that complaint. One way was to file "A Request to Staff Member" called a "cop-out." This form was available in several locations in the cellhouse or clothing room. The inmate would complete the form and drop it on the west end officer's desk. The inmate could address it to any of the various prison officials including the Warden, Associate Warden, Superintendent of Industries, MTA, etc. These officers would then investigate and respond back to the inmate.

Prison officials gave inmates GOOD TIME CREDIT meaning they got 1, 2 or 3 days credit for each day served. There were three types of good time credits: 1. Industries good time credit earned for working in industries; 2. Earned Good Time credit for obeying prison rules and regulations; and 3. Statutory Good Time for a sentence of ten years or more. In essence an inmate could get up to 3 days good time for each day served in the prison, thus allowing an inmate to significantly reduce his sentence. Good time credit could also be forfeited and added back to their sentence. An inmate could get out earlier with these earned credits but if they were forfeited they could only add time back on the sentence up to the amount of the initial sentence. If they had no good time credits, punishment such as withholding other privileges or segregation including the DARK HOLE would be awarded. An inmate could lose several of these at the same time.

A directive from the Bureau of Prisons issued in late 1961, early 1962, established an "institutional court" for the inmates. This new procedure required the prison to have court at the institution when rule violations, etc., were committed and before punishment was handed out. The inmate could request any guard at the prison to represent him at the court. Court was held in "A" Block. Each inmate was read his rights before his case was heard. One of the first court cases which I escorted the inmate to the court and remained until the court concluded, involved a "slipping out of his cell into another cell for sex."

A guard's daily routine was just as strictly controlled as the inmates. It was also highly regimented with little variations from day to day. One of the many tasks that never ended was the counting of the inmates. The frequency with which these "counts" were conducted was a constant complaint on the part of the inmates and even the guards. Each time there was a mass movement of inmates there was a count. They were counted about 16 times each day. Briefly summarized, part of the regular routine for an inmate was wake-up - count; breakfast - count; work call count census (while at work); return to cellhouse – count; lunch – count; sick call – count; work call count census (while at work); return to cellhouse – count; dinner – count; lock-up for the night. Four more official counts were taken by the guards throughout the evening hours and the guard was required to see "skin" and "breathing" while the inmate slept. During some counts, the Lieutenant would tell the West Gun Galley Guard he was ready for the count. The guard would push a button setting off the "ring" announcing the count. The guard at each cell block would then take count and inform the Lieutenant. When the count was OK, the Lieutenant would approve it and signal one long ring of the bell. Lieutenant Ordway would occasionally agitate the guards by saying "count it again." The cell guards would start the recount and get half finished when Ordway would ring the OK bell. I guess he wanted to see how the guards would react.

Many activities were started and stopped by the ringing of a bell. The West Gun Gallery guard had a button he would push to do this. For example, the bell would be set off for prisoner movements, wake-up, counts, sick call, and lights out.

The guards patrolled the cell block during the day and oversaw the work of orderlies cleaning the cell blocks. Guards, in all positions, who could possibly come in direct contact with inmates were unarmed and carried no keys. Keys could only be obtained, when needed, from the gun gallery by use of a rope. Each inmate was responsible for his cell and for keeping it clean and orderly. The inmate orderlies kept the aisles clean and polished. The aisles were wide and the inmates were very good at cleaning them. They would take a mop and going side-to-side do the whole aisle. Al Capone was one of the inmates who cleaned the floor of the cellhouse and, as I was told, the other inmates called him "the wop with the mop" but not to his face.

Sounds at night were interesting and included snoring, coughing, farting, toilets flushing, talking in sleep, wind whistling outside and the smell of smoke from cigarettes. Sometimes it was extremely quiet and that would occasionally bother me.

A guard had to always be on the alert and prepared for anything. During my very first watch as Acting Lieutenant on the 4:00 P.M. to midnight shift (on the two late shifts the Lieutenant is in control of the entire prison), the power on the entire island went off. This had never happened to me before and it startled me for obvious reasons. I was hoping for a quiet watch and thought to myself "what a way to start." I immediately sent the main gate officer to the back of the cellhouse (Tower #5) to watch the cellhouse. Within 40 minutes the power was restored and things got back to normal, so I thought. Shortly after things got back to normal, I assigned the Dock and Patrol Officer to shakedown the laundry and shoe repair facility of the Industries Building. Later in the evening when I went down to check on him he was opening the padlock leading to the shoe repair shop using lock picks, even though he had the keys. I asked him "what are you doing?" and he replied "I am taking a locksmith course and I am practicing." The rest of the shift went by without incident.

CHAPTER ELEVEN

The strict controls within the prison for inmates included every aspect of their life and involved their movements, eating, working, etc. The controls and restrictions were many and covered almost all of the things the rest of society takes as common in every day living. The inmates were very creative and found many ways to violate rules and regulations.

Radio jacks were installed in the cells after 1958 allowing inmates to listen to two different radio stations in their cells. These radio stations were monitored and censored by the guards in the control center or the west gun gallery. If someone was listening to music or a ball game and someone on the radio broke for a news report and it had something to do about inmates, Alcatraz, etc., the guard would shut down one or both of the stations. They were shut off at the 9:30 P.M. lights out.

Inmates were allowed seven magazines a month. The magazines were reviewed, censored, and edited for notorious articles/ads by the Main Gate Guard. If there was anything in the magazine, like a story on one of the inmates or about Alcatraz, etc., it would be cut out. A good example was when Mikey Cohen was coming to Alcatraz. He was a big time convict and a lot of articles were written about him. The guard would cut the article out of the magazine. An inmate would be reading a magazine and get to the end of page, say 24, which then referred him to say page 39. When he turned to page 39 that page could be missing because it contained part of the page that had the censored article.

Inmates could write two letters and receive 5-7 per week. All were censored; no sex, no violence, no mentioning of other inmates, etc., were allowed - the only exception to not being censored was letters sent to officials using the PMB (Prisoner's Mail Box) program. Mail coming in was received at the main gate and the main gate guard would censor the mail. After censoring he would send the mail into the cellhouse and the cellhouse officer would distribute it by delivering it directly to the cell and laying it between the bars. Letters from the inmates were also censored, except as noted above. The inmate had a form and envelope to use. On the top of the form was a tear off section which was removed by the main gate guard during the censoring process. The tear off section contained a record of whom and when letters were sent out, including address and was retained by the prison. I did the censoring several times and remember one instance when an inmate wrote a letter to his wife and also his girlfriend.

Telephones were not allowed in the cells and inmates were not allowed to make phone calls or receive phone calls. I wonder, with today's technology, what might have been allowed.

Contrary to belief, the inmates were allowed to have razor blades in their cells. They were exchanged weekly on Saturday. The evening watch cellhouse guard would, about 7:00 P.M., go around and put two double edge razor blades on the bar of the cell and pick-up two. Blades were closely watched inside the prison as well as in the private residence. There was no real worry about an inmate slicing his throat or wrist although that was a possibility; however it was his throat or wrist. Also we did not really worry about them possibly carrying them around as they went through metal detectors several times daily and at least weekly had to account for them. In the hospital they were given locking razors which had to be immediately returned after bath and shave. I only recall one instance of anyone cutting themselves with a razor blade. That occurred shortly after I arrived and although I didn't directly witness it, I did see some of the after effects. Several inmates decided to cut the tendons on their feet using a razor blade with the intent of avoiding segregation. They cut the tendons on their heels, got patched up and were put back in segregation.

Before 1961, inmates only had cold water available in their cells and had to wash and shave with cold water. Hot water baths were only available in the shower room and then at scheduled times, not daily. After 1961, hot water was made available to the inmates in their cells.

Every Monday, Wednesday and Friday the inmates received 1 pack of cigarettes. Inmates in segregation did not receive cigarettes or tobacco. The cigarettes were Wings, Kools, or Stradford. It depended on who got the contract as to what cigarettes were provided. The inmates could have one full pack and one open pack in their cell at any one time. They would hide more, as best they could, or pass them to someone to keep for them. The non-smokers took cigarettes as they could use them for money. Inmates could get just about anything they wanted with cigarettes; sex, hire someone to do something for them, etc. Cigarettes were money and inmates constantly had them hidden (they were good at this) in their cells. I had an incident when I was on duty in the cellhouse. I was letting the inmates out for chow and after the last one walked by I closed the cells and was going to check and find out who didn't go to eat and why. I went to the first cell and an inmate was in there. I stopped and said "OK, let's have them." I thought I saw someone put something in his cell as they went by, but I was not sure. He handed me a couple packs of cigarettes. I then said "I want them all." He gave me two cartons which I assume was a pay off on a debt.

At the end of each cell block there was a Bull Durham tobacco box, except D-Block, where tobacco was placed (Bull Durham,

Union Jack or George Washington) for rolling your own cigarettes or for use in pipes. Inmates could take all they wanted.

As the number and occasion to inspect cells reduced to almost none, it became easier for the inmates to hide cigarettes and other things.

At Alcatraz gambling was illegal and a violation of rules and regulations; however, inmates could and would gamble on just about anything. Inmates would bet on chess games, dominoes, etc. They would play chess/checkers with other prisoners in their cells by calling out numbers on the board to the nearby prisoner. Dominoes were very popular and many games were played. What was interesting was if an inmate had a dominant play he would jump up and slam the domino down.

Several educational programs were set up for the inmates and included English and Spanish language courses, crocheting, bridge and letter writing. An educational supervisor was hired in 1962.

Sex in Alcatraz was a most interesting part of an inmates life and took on many different forms, including masturbating, sneaking into another inmate's cell for sex, lovers, etc. Some was consensual and some forced. Fights sometimes occurred over lover quarrels. The inmates were locked up in individual cells, were closely supervised, and had very little time to be creative; however, as strict and controlled as things were, the inmates found ways to make things happen. There were several homosexuals in the prison; however, just because an inmate might want or engage in sex didn't necessarily mean they were homosexual. After being in prison for a time they got what they could get and wanted. I was on duty in the West End Gallery Guard when a guard came out of the restroom on C-Block and stepped around the corner and motioned to me to look at some cells. I eased over and could see a hand going in and out and in and out of one cell into another. He was having hand sex with the other prisoner. When they saw my shadow on the wall they quit.

There was an inmate who was a rather tall and thin individual. He was in the hospital and I caught him performing oral sex on himself!

Another incident concerned an inmate nicknamed "Peaches" and another inmate, Blakley. Peaches wanted to be a "she." When the cells for meals are opened they remain open for about 15 seconds and the inmates step out, file by and go to the dining room. The guard would then lock the cell doors. There was just enough time for Peaches to slip into another inmate's cell before the door closed. After the inmates filed into the dining room, the guard would look down the range to see if everyone went to chow. An inmate did not have to go to chow and could remain in his cell. If an inmate did not go to eat the guard would go and find out why. Some would say "not hungry boss" or I don't feel good", etc. I don't know if what they were saying was true or not but their reasons were believable. Anyway, the guard walked down the range and found Peaches sitting on inmate Blakley's lap on the toilet, having sex. It was hard to hide in a 5 X 9 cell. Both were put in the dark hole and a misconduct report was written.

Throughout my 4 years there were frequent and varying degrees of violence and disruption caused by the inmates. These included: fights with some more violent than others and included fists, knives, scissors, shovel handle, homosexual/lover quarrels, and nuisances such as making homemade firecrackers out of match heads and tape, lighting them and throwing them out in the cell block where they exploded. They also would on occasion blow their toilets up by lighting paper and rags in the toilet and then turning the water on. An average of 12 disciplinary reports were turned in monthly by the guards. Many of these resulted in forfeiture of good time.

Work was a privilege and was not a full eight hour day as we know it. By the time they ate, were counted, sick call, etc., they might work from 8:30 A.M. until 11:30 A.M.; come back-in, another count, lunch, sick call, another count and back out around 1:10 P.M. and work until about 3:30 P.M. before coming back-in for the day. Additionally on Tuesday, shower day, they would stop working approximately one and a half hours early to go to their cell and go to the shower and clothing area. The inmates were assigned work grades (1, 2, or 3) for which they received hourly wages based upon hours worked. I believe Grade 3 paid 10 cents per hour; grade

2 paid 13 or 15 cents an hour; and grade 1 paid 22 cents per hour. Inmates on work details received breaks and were allowed to smoke but only in designated areas.

There was a small canteen/store for inmates; however, they were limited with what they could buy and prior approval was required. Initially only such items as art and painting supplies were approved. As the rules were lessened they were allowed to purchase other things such as tennis shoes, etc. Cigarettes, candy, etc., could not be purchased.

Before my time there was an inmate who was an artist. Story has it that he was resentful toward prison authorities supposedly because they took his art stuff from him and wouldn't let him continue his art. He worked in the model shop, got an ax to trim wood and instead decided to chop off the fingers on one of his hands. The inmate's minds are a lot different than mine, and even more reason we had to be extremely careful and watchful.

Sick call was held every day at noon, right after lunch. If an inmate was sick in the morning he had to be sick until noon; however, if an inmate was really hurting the MTA (Medical Technician Assistant) would look at him in his cell. After lunch the inmates would go to their cells, get counted and if they wanted to go to sick call would proceed to the first line on Broadway and wait for their turn. They were let out one tier at a time. Sick call started three quarters of the way up Broadway facing the dining room. There was a line on the floor and the inmates would all line up on that line. A second line on the floor was right in front of the dining room entrance and faced north. A third line on Times Square was directly in front of a temporary table where the medical technician was located. The inmates would proceed to each of these lines when called and the MTA would hold sick call, dispense drugs, etc. When completed the inmates would go back to their cells. If they were really sick they would be escorted to the hospital. The MTA kept them moving, sick, lame and lazy. In some instances the MTA may issue a lay-in where the inmate would go back to his cell and be locked in, then after work call the inmate would be escorted to the hospital to be seen again by the MTA. When sick call was over and everyone returned to his cell, that was considered a major movement, and an official count was taken. Once this was completed the inmates would go to their respective jobs. The MTA would then proceed to segregation in D-Block to hold sick call. He went to each cell.

Holidays and special occasions were generally pretty quiet with maybe a few extra visitors. At Christmas, the industries would give the inmates a Christmas package containing such things as an apple, orange, small candy, couple cigars and maybe a pack of Camel cigarettes. This was big money for them and everybody got one. Some inmates did not smoke but they took what they were given as it made for good trading or money items for them. A special holiday menu was published each Christmas. The menu reflected the activities for Christmas Eve and Christmas day and listed the food for Christmas dinner. The back of the menu contained a list of the Prison Administration Officials.

To celebrate the New Year, some of the inmates made their own fireworks. They would make bombs out of matches and explode them making loud noises.

Meals were extra special during holidays and appreciated by the inmates. For example: On Veterans Day 1959, inmates were served a steak dinner and then listened to the football game in the afternoon over the radio. On Memorial Day 1962, dinner consisted of T-bone steak, French fries and all the trimmings.

Being locked in individual cells caused inmates to figure out ways to communicate or pass information to other inmates. Some used toilets as telephones and to pass material from floor to floor. The cellhouse consisted of 3 main corridors each with 3 tiers of cells. If an inmate wanted to pass something to the inmate directly below him he would place it in the toilet and flush the stool. The inmate in the cell below him would reach up the toilet pipe and catch the item. As a telephone they would put a blanket over their head and talk into the toilet to those above or below; not a private line. Others would pass small notes or cigarettes from cell to cell through the use of cockroaches. An inmate in one cell would catch a cockroach and tie a cigarette to its back with a piece of thread. The inmate a few cells down would place a piece of bread outside his cell knowing the cockroach would run for it. Mirrors were used to view outside the cell and were used to alert others when a guard was making his round or approaching.

There were no town meetings but with 260 inmates it was easy to pass the word. You would tell 2 or 3 and everyone knows. A speaker system that could address everyone including the island residents and inmates, or just specific areas, was available for broader use as required.

Most prisoners called guards by "Mr." or "boss." They did not use first names. They did, however, use other less favorable names such as "screw," "hacks," and "bulls."

Regardless of how thorough inspections were conducted, inmates would always find ways to get things that could be used as a weapon or tool. They not only had plenty of time to think of ways to do this but had access to areas within the prison where wood, metal, etc., was available, such as in the industries. All they had to do was figure a way to get it through the detectors or into their cell. There was always someone to help or to whom a debt was owed.

In February 1961, a homemade bar spreader was found in the brush shop. It was made from a piece of pipe, threaded bolt and a piece of "C" clamp. It had to be made during working hours in the shop. The inmates probably intended to return this to the cellhouse via the laundry hampers which must be cleared at the dock before being brought up to the cellhouse. The inmate who made this spreader was never discovered.

CHAPTER TWELVE

There were only a few well known or glamorized inmates who served time on the ROCK. Most of the inmates were not that famous. Those who were well known were some of the most notorious and vicious criminals of their time. However, although these prisoners were famous outside the prison walls, they were just minor role players within the strict confines of Alcatraz. Movies have been made about many of them including Robert Stroud (The Birdman of Alcatraz) (AZ 594); Al "Scarface" Capone (AZ 85); George "Machine Gun" Kelly (AZ 117); Alvin "Creepy" Karpis (AZ 325); Arthur R. "Doc" Barker (AZ 268) who was a son of Ma Barker; and the Anglin Brothers (John and Clarence) who along with Frank Morris made one of the most publicized escapes on June 11, 1962. The majority of the inmates sent to Alcatraz were because they refused to conform to the rules and regulations at other Federal institutions, etc. The stories and history of most of the "famous" inmates have been published or told many times; however, all 1,576 inmates who were in the prison at one time or another (some more than once) brought their own unique problem, background and behavioral attitudes. Some created a challenge for the guards and others just quietly spent their time. Some of the human interest stories concerned less famous inmates and are worth noting; they reflect on the background and mind set of just a few.   BUMPY JOHNSON (AZ 1117): Bumpy, an African-American, was the Al Capone of Harlem. He spent several different periods in Alcatraz. He was looked at by the other African-American inmates as their leader and spent time in the yard sitting on the bleachers. He sat high in the bleachers, a sign of authority and power. I remember him getting a visitor one particular day and suddenly starting to laugh. Then he said "Mr. Albright, did you hear what this man asked me, "He asked me if anyone at Alcatraz was crazy." I asked Bumpy what his response was to the man and he responded: "Hell, I told him we were all crazy!" I liked Bumpy and had no problems with him. He was one that other prisoners did not cross and he could get other inmates things, for a price.

SAM TIBLOW (AZ 1265) worked in the trash and greenhouse areas. The greenhouse was located outside the yard below Tower #2. Sam kept a pet mouse on a chain and the mouse would sit on his shoulders. He kept it in his cell and carried it under his coat collar. One day the mouse was missing and presumed dead. Sam's cell was next to Mickey Cohen's cell; and Cohen, being a neat freak and not particularly fond of mice, was afraid the mouse would get in his cell at night. Thus, was a contract put out on the mouse or was this another escape from Alcatraz?

ARCHIE LYLES (AZ 1321) died in prison of a heart attack, but there was no sympathy. One of the inmates asked me what happened to Archie and I explained to him that he had a heart attack and died. The inmate replied "The SOB really beat the government out of a lot of time."

DULWORTH (AZ 1382) AND HIS "DOG": Dulworth was always calling for his "dog" to follow him around. The MTA told him there was a treatment (electrical shock) for people who were going crazy. Dulworth quickly straightened out and said "The hell you are, I'm not any crazier than you. I just wanted a change of scenery". Dulworth just wanted to be transferred to the hospital cell. He was sent back to his regular cell but to the best of my knowledge still kept the dog.

MICKEY COHEN (AZ 1518): In July 1961, the "famous" or "infamous" Mickey Cohen was received under the name of Meyer H. Cohen. He worked for me in the clothing room. I talked with him before he came down to work for me in the clothing room and said to him, "You know we are going to go right across the board and follow all the rules" and I said "if you try anything different your job is gone." He was a clean freak and wanted to shower daily. I told him "as long as you work for me and do your job you can have a shower every day; however, if you cross me you are gone and there goes your shower." He had the opportunity to have a shower every day because he worked for me and I ran the clothing room and shower room. His job was sorting clothes. He would take a shower just before getting off work. He would take his shower by himself or sometimes when other inmates were showering. I allowed him to shower because we had showers every day anyway as the kitchen workers would come down and shower. I also felt this would make him a better inmate. Other than allowing him to shower daily, Cohen was treated like everyone else. I couldn't say he was a model prisoner because we don't always know what is going on behind the scenes, but he was very respectful of every officer and said "yes sir, no sir", things like that. He was good in that sense. He was a leader in prison among the inmates and a lot of the young inmates wanted to get close to him for that reason. Some of the inmates resented him.

Being a neat freak he was very clean. Everything had to be just so so. He had clean clothes because he worked in the clothing room and he kept them clean. One time we got new mattresses for everybody in the institution. One of the young inmates offered to carry Cohen's new mattress up to his cell. He got the mattress and took it up to the 2nd tier at the west end on the outside of B Block as that was where Cohen's cell was. The inmate hung it over the rail waiting for them to open the cell. Cohen came unglued, he thought that the mattress was filthy from hanging it on the rail that everyone put their hands on. He was fanatic about it. He wanted a new one but he did not get one. He had to get it from me and I told him that it is tough. He got out on bail on October 17, 1961, for a short period of time and was returned in May 1962. When they closed the prison he was transferred to the prison in Atlanta. He only served a short period on Alcatraz, about 1 ½ years.

Story has it that an inmate named McDONALD (AZ 1542), who was in Alcatraz the same time as Cohen, was transferred to Atlanta when the prison closed. McDonald crawled over a fence at the Atlanta prison, which separated the yards and beat Cohen's head in. They said it was a case of mistaken identity. I have a hard time believing that. Cohen was in Alcatraz with 260 other prisoners and he worked in the clothing room. McDonald saw him at least twice a week when he came down to shower. There is no mistaken identify. He knew who it was. He didn't kill Cohen but definitely was trying to.

FRANK SPRENZ (AZ 1414) was the infamous 'FLYING BANDIT." He was on the FBI's 10 most wanted list for bank robbery. He would rob a bank then go to an airport, steal a small plane and escape. He really didn't know how to fly and wrecked several small planes in attempts to get away. When the island closed and I was escorting a chain of inmates to another prison, which included Frank, another inmate told me to tell the pilot not to worry because if anything happened Frank would fly the plane. The thought of an inmate flying this plane with me aboard wasn't the best feeling. I once escorted him to "Institutional Court" for refusing to work.

TAMOYA KAWAKITA—aka, "Meatball" (AZ 1059): Meatball was Japanese and an American citizen. When the war with Japan broke out he went back to Japan and was involved in torturing American prisoners of war. After the war he came back to the states and a prisoner of war he had tortured recognized him walking down the streets of Los Angeles and reported him to authorities. He was sent to Alcatraz. He wanted to be returned to Japan and the Japanese government intervened on his behalf and he was returned to Japan. He was a very good worker with no problems.

ALVIN FRANCIS KARPOVICK (AZ 325) better known as ALVIN "CREEPY' KARPIS). The first Public enemy #1, he spent 26 years on Alcatraz. He was a member of Ma Barker's gang. When the prison closed he was transferred to the U.S. Penitentiary at McNeil Island in April 1962. He was subsequently released and deported to Canada in l969. He committed suicide in Spain in 1979.

ELMER ANTHONY "KEMO" MERRILL (AZ 1158) was an Alaskan inmate who was locked up three times for raping the same woman three separate times. He raped her and got 2 years; was released went back and raped her again and got 3 years; got released and went back and raped her again and got 5 years.

GEORGE MCCOY (AZ 1205) and FRANK HATFIELD (AZ 1296) were descendants of "feuding" families, the Hatfield's and McCoy's. There was no feuding in Alcatraz and they created no problems.

LEON "WHITEY" THOMPSON (AZ 1465): After his release he raised wolves and has written several books on Alcatraz. I have talked to Whitey several times at subsequent Alcatraz reunions.

JAMES CLARK (AZ 242) was the lowest number inmate when I started as a guard at Alcatraz in 1959.

CHAPTER THIRTEEN

What does one usually think about when the words dining room are mentioned? A quiet, peaceful place to relax and enjoy a good meal or a very dangerous place. At Alcatraz, the answer was obvious. This was one of the few places that all the inmates were together, three different times daily. They were in relatively close quarters, with each issued a fork, cup and bowl, all made of metal!

The dining room, kitchen and bakery were located in the same area but sectioned off. Entrance to these areas was by the West end of the cell blocks. It was one of the few places I had limited duty, although I occasionally relieved other guards. On one occasion I served a short assignment during the inmate work stoppage (strike) in 1961.

Three squares were one of the few guarantees an inmate had at Alcatraz. It probably was not worth going to Alcatraz for, but the food was considered quite good and not only varied but had flavor. It was nutritious but not overly expensive. In prison, good food made for better order. Serving a variety and sufficient quantity helped eliminate problems. Menus were posted daily before each meal.

Inmates would be counted prior to entering the dining room. They would enter by cell block tier, in single file; pick-up a tray which had food compartments, a bowl, and a cup – all metal. Tables in the dining room were rather large and seated 10 men to a table. Ten sets of forks and spoons – all metal – were previously arranged on each table. After July 1961, the 10 man tables were replaced with tables that seated only 4. This was well received by the inmates but made it harder for the guards to supervise the inmates and keep track of the utensils. Inmates were allowed approximately 20 minutes to eat.

Security was extremely tight and all movements were strictly controlled. In addition to the guards who were stationed in the dining room, usually 10, an armed guard was on duty in the dining room cage. He patrolled outside the dining room windows which had no access to the dining room. This guard had a pistol and carbine; could alert the control center of an emergency and, if necessary, had the means to release tear gas. An emergency alarm button was located in a box within the cage, which the guard could use to alert the control center. Also, a button was available to release tear gas to different sections of the dining room. The dining room cage was only manned during meal times. The guard in the West Gun Gallery was also available as a back-up during meal periods.

When the meal was completed they would place their cups upside down on the table and would leave all eating utensils - tray, bowl, cup, fork and spoon - on the table for the guard on duty to inspect. The guard could easily count 10 trays, 10 cups, 10 forks, 10 bowls, and 10 spoons. When he was satisfied that everything was accounted for he then dismissed the inmates. They left in the same manner they had entered, by cell block tier. As they exited, in single file, they went through a metal detector. While they were leaving the guard kept a very close eye on the utensils that were still on the table as inmates were constantly looking for opportunities to get anything they could use for either a weapon or for other purposes. They returned to their cells where another mass count was taken.

Inmates occasionally argued and fought or created other problems in the dining room.

In February 1961, two inmates removed the handles of garbage cans to stab each other. In March 1960, an inmate assaulted another inmate with a home made knife.

One of the more comical incidents involved an inmate named Hubbard. When he got to the large 20 gallon kool aid container (inmates filled their cup using a dipper), he laid his tray down, picked up the container and began drinking the whole thing. Kool aid was all over the place and Hubbard was completely covered, head to toe. Several of the guards on duty immediately grabbed him and escorted him to the hospital where he was placed in the bug cage - an observation cell.

Another incident, which was not comical, involved two inmates who worked in the kitchen. One of the inmates (called Wolf) was pressuring the other inmate for sex. The inmate being pressured didn't take it too well. Somehow he got a piece of metal pipe, which I believe came from a dishwasher, and smashed Wolf on the head causing very serious damage and leaving him in a vegetative state. Wolf was subsequently transferred to the Bureau of Prison Medical Hospital in Springfield, Missouri. I specifically remember Wolf as he was an extremely strong individual who enjoyed flexing his muscles when being searched.

Another incident occurred in the dining room during the Christmas holiday season. A Christmas tree, decorated with ornaments and lights, was set-up in the dining room. As the inmates entered at meal time, one of the inmates walked over to the tree, knocked it down, picked-it up, and began to drag it out of the dining room. He never did explain why. He was immediately escorted to segregation.

A new officer, Charles Hermann, who was at Alcatraz for about three days, was touring the dining room with several other new officers. Officer Jerry Herring, a guard in the dining room/kitchen, had one of the inmate clerks help him pull a prank on Officer Hermann. Officer Herring told the clerk that when he gave him the high sign he wanted the inmate to come out of the office (cubicle in the middle of the kitchen which was surrounded by glass and was used as an office) yelling and screaming. Officer Herring was walking around with the new guards, gave the inmate the high sign and the inmate came out yelling and screaming. Officer Hermann turned around and ran out of the dining room. This was Officer Herring's way of testing to see how a guard reacted. Later Officer Hermann ended up working in the kitchen.

Few inmates complained about the food; however, there were occasions when agitators would cause disruptions or create problems. In June 1960, several agitators put pressure on other inmates to complain about the food and as a result, due to fear, only 29 inmates went to the dining room. We didn't care if they ate or not, but had to keep a sharp eye on the agitators in case they had anything else in mind.

Inmates working in the kitchen preparing meals and cleaning were supervised by a Food Service Supervisor. Cleanliness was demanded and the kitchen and dining areas were spotless. Those who worked in the kitchen got extra chow and that was an outstanding privilege. Part of the inmate cook's responsibility included handling large butcher knives. These knives were stored in a cabinet called the "shadow board." The shadow board cabinet contained an opening for every knife and that opening was painted with the shape of the knife so that each knife had its own slot. This allowed a guard to quickly glance and see if anything was missing.

Inmates in Alcatraz had very diverse ethnic backgrounds. As such, some wouldn't eat beef and others wouldn't eat pork as it was against their religious convictions. There was enough variation in food so that everyone was satisfied. If an inmate in segregation acted up the officer would purposely serve them what they knew they wouldn't eat, or food they didn't like. When they took it to them in their cell the inmate would usually throw it back at them. The guard would then write in his report "Inmate refused to eat for unknown reason."

While everyone heard about the escape attempts, very few know about the seven-day "work (stoppage) strike" that occurred in 1961. The inmates refused to work and would not come out of their cells at work call. They were striking because they felt they weren't being compensated properly for the work they performed. They wanted more money. I believe at that time they were being paid ten cents an hour. During the first hours of the strike, the administration using shop supervisors, some Lieutenants and a few of the officers, went from cell to cell and interviewed each inmate. They asked "Do you want to go to work, tell me yes or no, either refuse or step out?" The plan was to get someone to break the ice. It didn't work! Pressure from other inmates was too great. Only the dock crew and two hospital orderlies went to work. As the strike continued it was determined that a few strong agitators started it and were keeping it going.

An inmate, Gino Scusselle (AZ 1356), created quite a stir when they opened the cell doors to let anyone out who wanted to work and he was the only one on the range to step out. He was a strappy, strong inmate who exercised and lifted weights. I think he held the record for the dead lift in the 181 pound class. He also was a very hard working inmate. Well, someone down the range yelled something and Scusselle walked down the range, stood in front of one of the cells, grabbed the bars and said something, We couldn't hear what he said; however, from then on whenever he came out of his cell to work, no words were said. The cell doors were opened every day to allow anyone who wanted to work to come out.

Although on strike, the inmates had to eat and I believe the food had a lot to do with the strike coming to a good ending. They were fed fantastic sandwiches which were made by an assembly line process by the officers in the bakery. I called them fantastic because I helped make them. The bread was laid out a couple of hours before lunch. Peanut Butter was dropped on the bread by spoon, likewise the jelly. Sandwiches were made, wrapped and put in a sack for each inmate. Egg sandwiches were the other fantastic sandwiches we served.

Making fried egg sandwiches was quite an experience for me. Learning to crack the eggs with one hand was both an opportunity for me to learn something new and also a challenge. I had a hell of a time with this. The food services supervisor would grab an egg in each hand, crack them with the egg going into the pot and the shells being thrown in the garbage. I tried this, one hand would work but the other would mash the shell and the pieces would fall into the pot. After some close instructions from the supervisor I finally got the hang of it. At first I would try to remove the pieces of shell that fell in the pot; however, the supervisor told me "Hell no, don't worry about that. They aren't going to hurt nothing, and we are going to grind them up anyway when we scramble them and they need the calcium."

Inmates were fed only two meals a day during the strike and the sacks were literally thrown in the cells. The first meal, peanut butter and jelly sandwiches, was delivered to the cells but some inmates threw them out. That stopped after a couple of days when they started to get hungry and from then on they ate. They were not provided anything special to drink. Water was available in their cells and that was what they used; however, some of the more creative inmates made what they called "stingers." It was against the rules to make the stingers but they did anyway. They would attach a metal spoon or other metal object to a wire, attach the wire to their light fixture causing the metal spoon or object to get hot. They would then place the hot metal spoon or other metal object in water heating the water. If they had some coffee grounds, which they may have stolen or procured from the kitchen earlier, they could make coffee. I thought about where they got the wire and metal objects and where they hid them in the cell. It just goes to show how smart and creative these people could be and made me even more cautious and alert.

No movement occurred during the strike days. No clean clothes, no movies, no church, nothing, including showers. Some would wash in their sink with the water that was available to them in their cells. They could shave but the blades quickly got dull. They were not issued new blades during the strike. Some started to get ripe. The few inmates who worked ate regular meals and were given changes in clothes, etc.

Cell doors were opened daily for a short period of time to allow anyone who wanted to work to come out. Prison officials would go around and interview the inmates, asking them if they wanted to come out and work. Some would say "I'm ready to go back to work boss" but wouldn't. After 7 days of no showers, not eating in the dining room and just having those delicious sandwiches to eat, questions and concerns from the inmates began to change. We would go around talking to them. I would ask them "What's going on?" and they would reply "Just sitting here reading." When asked "Are you ready to go back to work" a common reply was "I am but I don't want to be the first one. I won't be the first, but if someone steps out I'll go." Finally we were able to identify several inmates who we were pretty sure were the agitators. They were locked up in segregation. Once this occurred, the other inmates broke and went back to work. The strike was over without a change in the wage structure. Needless to say the inmates ate heartily at their first meal in the dining room.

Four of the inmates who cooperated with the institution to the extent they worked each day during the work stoppage were transferred to other institutions. This was a fair reward for proper conduct and probably kept them safe.

The guards ate the same food as the inmates, and I might say the food was excellent. A side note – we did not eat any egg and peanut butter and jelly sandwiches. When I first started the officer's mess was in the back of the kitchen. Later, an officer's mess was built upstairs directly above the warden's office. Entry was through the main gate. Guards had to pay for their meals and purchased meal tickets. The cost was .25 cents per meal which later was raised to .35 cents.

CHAPTER FOURTEEN

Directly above the dining room was the one place I didn't enjoy going to, the hospital.

Access was strictly controlled and just getting there was a chore. Immediately as you entered the dining room, to your left, was a locked door that started the journey. After getting the keys and unlocking the door you proceeded up a flight of stairs to the second floor and another locked door. Once in the stairway, between the two locked doors, it was just you and whomever might be with you. In essence you were trapped. The guard on duty in the hospital, which was manned 24 hours a day, would then open the second locked door thus allowing access into the hallway which led into the hospital ward. Finally you are there.

The hospital ward was a large room containing 3 large cells on each side with 4 beds in each cell. The last ward on the left side contained a sink and bathtub where inmates could shave and bathe. All wards were lockable and in most instances only one inmate was assigned per ward.

The hospital was fully equipped with an X-ray machine, physical therapy apparatus, laboratories and dental equipment. It was staffed with an MTA, a career medical technician of the Public Health Service. He lived on top of the island near the Warden's home. Inmate orderlies were assigned to the hospital ward to assist during the day time.

Shortly after training, I was assigned to supervise the hospital. At that time there were 5 inmate patients, 3 down the right side and 2 on the left. Being new I referred to the job analysis sheet which would outline what and when things had to be done. I noticed that Wednesdays were bath days and I was responsible for bathing them. I remember thinking "What a thrill!" On that day, among the inmates was a rather large African-American, named Sam. He was as gruff as could be. He was just served his meal when all of a sudden a loud crash was heard. Sam threw his tray with the food out of his ward's cell. I went over and said "Sam, what is the matter." He replied "The tray fell, the bones and all." He felt the meat had too many bones in it. That incident was the only trouble I ever had with Sam, although other guards had trouble with him. Well, its Wednesday and bath day so I say to Sam, "Sam are you ready for a bath." He stated "Yes, sir boss." I opened his ward, escorted him across to the bathing cell, opened it, he went in and I handed him a locking razor. I locked the cell and told him to give me a yell when he was done. I left and shortly thereafter he yelled and I went over and escorted him back to his ward. I went ahead and did three more of the inmates with only one remaining to bathe. It was now lunch time and I was relieved. I went down to the cellhouse for lunch and Lieutenant Rennenberg stopped me and said "Mr. Albright today is Wednesday and bath day at the hospital."

I told him "Yes Sir, I know, I am all done except for one." He went right straight up in the air.

"You what!"

I stated "I got them all done, but one." He said "You are to have help, not do it by yourself." After he calmed down he said "I will send you some help for the last one." He sent me another guard; however, he was very little help.

There were some interesting stories of inmates in the hospital. One of those stories involved an inmate with a metal plate in his head. He was also a little goofy. On one occasion he was running across the room hitting his head on the wall. Lieutenant Ordway went up and was going to put a stop to this activity. He grabbed the inmate, who in turn grabbed Lieutenant Ordway by the testicles. Well, Ordway let out a horrible scream and the inmate let go. Later Lieutenant Ordway asked him "You had me why did you let me go?" The inmate replied: "When I heard you scream I knew how it felt. I had to let go."

Also on the 2nd floor but on the opposite end of the cellhouse from the hospital and directly above the Warden's office, was the movie and chapel room. It was one room that was used for both purposes.

Inmates were only allowed to go to the movies on weekends; one half of the inmates on Saturday and the other half on Sunday. They didn't have to go and most of the time only about 30-40 went. If they did not go to the movies or to the yard when authorized, they would be locked in their cell until the next morning for breakfast. Movies were rented from a movie company in San Francisco and were picked up and returned weekly. They were screened before being shown. A list of movies was published and inmates voted on what they wanted to see. The one checked the most was rented first. During the movie the biggest trouble was smoking. They were not allowed to smoke; however, they would try. The inmates would smoke in such a manner that you could not see the fire; however, they couldn't hide the smoke or the smell of cigarettes. Other than that there were few problems. This was another way to get out of their cell and it helped reduce the boredom. The movies shown were the type with actresses such as Shirley Temple. The East Gun Gallery was manned when movies were being shown.

Worship services were held each Sunday. Chaplains also visited the prison during the week. One inmate got religion (as they all seem to do) while behind bars. As such, he talked a priest into coming to visit him every Sunday. Inmates requesting to see a priest, rabbi, minister, etc., were taken out of their cells and sat at the East

End officer's desk to meet. The inmate would bum cigarettes off the priest. On one particular Sunday the priest came in to see the inmate and I told him to go visit the inmate outside his cell. When the priest arrived at the inmate's cell the inmate suddenly lost his religion as he was only interested in the priest to get him out of his cell and give him some cigarettes.

The clothing room and shower area was located in the basement below the main cellhouse. A senior officer was assigned to the clothing room, as it was one of the more responsible positions. This was one of my favorite positions. I had the opportunity to be assigned, by the Captain, for 3 straight quarters (approximately 9 months). The clothing room was a caged area and contained a large number of bins with numbers on them. The numbers corresponded to the number written in an inmates clothing. Several inmate orderlies were assigned to work inside the cage. When an inmate was leaving the island (e.g., parole, transfer, court appearance, etc.) the Clothing Officer was responsible for arranging the clothing that the inmate would be wearing. Normally the inmate clerk would leave a list of transfers on my desk. At about 3:30 A.M the inmate to be transferred would be escorted from his cell to the dining room for breakfast and then down to the clothing room to be readied for transfer. Here he was strip searched (including body cavities), dressed, cuffed, leg-ironed, and belly chained before being escorted to the boat for the trip to Fort Mason.

The clothing room was also known for its excitement. On one occasion (just before I arrived) an inmate, Roland Eugene Simcox (AZ 1131), got into an argument with his best friend on Alcatraz (another inmate). His friend spit in Roland's face and Roland responded by stabbing him to death with a home made instrument. Roland was a particularly troublesome inmate as he started with 6 months in the stockade at Leavenworth and worked his time up to 42 ½ years in prison for assaulting officers and other inmates.

The shower area, which was communal, was located in the middle of an open room directly in front of the clothing room. I could easily observe the inmates showering; however, when the inmates showered, 6-8 additional guards were present to observe and control the showering process.

Inmates showered twice weekly, once on Tuesday afternoon when they were released from work 1 ½ hours early and then again on Saturday morning. They were escorted to the showers from their cells by tier. When one tier was done, the Lieutenant would call the cellhouse officer and another tier would be sent. When they came down the stairs, some would be in robes and some only in their shorts. There would be about 36 inmates there at any one time. The inmates deposited their soiled clothing in barrels, one by one, as an officer made sure an exact amount of clothing was deposited. After taking a shower the inmates would come to the clothing room window and receive 3 days worth of clean clothing. The clean clothing came from the island's own laundry facility.

A band room, a small room (old storage area) was located next to the clothing room and inmates were allowed to play musical instruments every Saturday. Inmates owned their instruments and kept them in their cells. I occasionally supervised the inmates in the band room and the music sometimes would drive me nuts.

A barber shop was located at the end of A-Block. It was a small room with two barber chairs. Inmates got haircuts once a month. They were escorted to and from their cells. Fellow inmates would do the cutting with close supervision by guards. Also, new inmates received their first haircut and shave immediately after arriving on the island. Before I arrived at Alcatraz, inmates were not issued razors in their cells thus they would go to the barber shop for shaves. This was also closely supervised as a straight razor was used to do the shaving. I was told by an inmate that on one of the shave days an inmate was getting a hair cut and shave by another inmate named Curly Thomas. These two inmates were apparently lovers; however the inmate getting the shave had recently broken up with Curly. Curly decided to do a good job on his ex-lover and when he completed the shave he asked him if he did a good job and if he was happy. The inmate replied yes he was. At that time Curly took the straight razor and slit the throat of his ex-lovers and bent over and kissed him. The inmate died.

Another incident involved a new inmate named Doyle. He had just been given his haircut and Lieutenant Ordway said that it wasn't close enough and he had the barber cut Doyle's hair shorter. When Doyle got up and out of the chair he hit Lieutenant Ordway right in the mouth. Doyle was escorted to segregation.

Located in the main cellhouse and at the end of D-Block was the library. It was open Monday through Friday, 8 A.M. to 4 P.M. A Library attendant, who was a wage board employee, was assigned and had several inmate orderlies assist him. Reading was one of the few diversions available to the inmate in his cell until lights out at 9:30 P.M. The library contained a store of books and magazines. Inmates had library cards and a list of books in their cells. To order a book, an inmate would submit a request slip with his library card and drop it in a box at the entrance to the dining hall at breakfast. A library orderly would bring the requested books to the inmate's cell during the day. An inmate was allowed 5 books in his cell at any one time; in addition to a Bible, dictionary, and text books. This was a privilege which could be taken away. Books were screened for sex, violence or crime. The library subscribed to several magazines which were censored. Prisoners were allowed to pay for subscriptions to selected magazines. These were also censored by prison officials when they arrived. The inmates would share magazines with their friends.

Warden Blackwell reported to the Director, Bureau of Prisons that during May 1962, a much needed shakedown and bar inspection was conducted. During this shakedown two books were found in the library that had been carved out in the center and contained several items of contraband, including a knife.

CHAPTER FIFTEEN

No firearms, of any kind, were allowed within the confines of the main cellhouse. The outside guard positions that had weapons required a special sense of responsibility and accountability. I remember saying to myself "What would I do and at what point do I do it?" when confronted with the situation of whether to shoot or not. I was a pretty good marksman and I thank God that I never had a situation occur where I had to make that decision and apply that skill.

The only armed guards within the main cellhouse were those who manned the two inside caged gun galleries. One was located at the West end of the cellhouse and was manned seven days a week, 24 hours. The other was located at the East end of the cellhouse and was only manned during meals, church and movies. The guards were only armed with gas guns. The 1946 riots started in the West end gun gallery when inmates crawled up into the gallery through the bars because rifles and pistols were kept in the gun gallery at that time. Subsequent to the riot, all fire arms were removed from inside the building and detention sashes were installed over the bars of the galleries. If keys were needed for any purpose in the main cellhouse, they were issued by the west end gun gallery. The keys would be lowered on a rope to the guard.

To get to the west gun gallery required walking around the outside of the building on a metal catwalk. Just before coming to the rear cellhouse door, the main gate officer would open another door to let the guards enter to go to their posts.

I was on duty as the West Gun Gallery officer during the 4 p.m. to midnight shift. One of my duties was to periodically check on the segregation officer in cell Block-D. As I made by rounds I saw the guard playing chess with one of the inmates in segregation. The board was on the floor in front of the inmate's cell. With the lights on all night it made it very easy to see. The guard was squatting down, would make a move on the board, leave to do his duties, return and continue the game.

To make sure guards were always on the alert, the Lieutenant would use his flashlights to flash the guards. The guard would see the flash of light and then flash back acknowledging that he did in fact see the flash. This was done inside the cellhouse as well as at the guards who were outside in the towers. On one incident the Lieutenant flashed the West gun gallery guard and got no response. He then went up to the second level of the cell block where he could see across and into the gun gallery. He again flashed the gun gallery and again got no response. He proceeded to the third level where he could look down. He had no response and could not see the guard. Being very concerned he got the main gate guard and they opened the door and the Lieutenant entered the gun gallery. What he found was frightening! There lying on the floor, sound asleep, was the guard with a big sign that read "I quit." The Lieutenant woke the guard and had a relief take the watch. I recall thinking "Why didn't he just up and quit? What would have happened if a serious situation occurred and he was needed?"

The East Gun Gallery was accessed by going through the officer's mess. I always walked as close to the building as I could when on the catwalk "just in case" something happened to the catwalk. It wasn't in very good shape and was getting pretty flimsy. This deterioration was caused by the salt air, which was abundant.

When I first arrived at Alcatraz, shakedowns and security checks of cells, bars, the cellhouse and other areas in the prison were conducted on a routine basis, almost daily. Different areas were inspected at different times. The guards would go through these areas and try to find contraband or things that weren't or didn't seem right. Being young, energetic and stout I would crawl like a monkey on the bars and would hit them with a rubber hammer. If the bars were cut at all, a different sound would be heard. When the prison system started getting into money problems, help was cut, and the frequency of the checks was significantly reduced to spot checks only. Inmates cleaned their own cells, and as we know from the 1962 escape involving the Anglin Brothers and Morris, they were good at hiding things. The frequent security checks and shakedowns of cells and other locations were a definite deterrent to the inmates. The inmates could see the lessening of controls and I am sure this gave them more incentive and more opportunity to be creative and think of ways to hide things and plan an escape.

Personal shakedowns of prisoners also occurred frequently whenever something suspicious occurred or was suspected. Sometimes just to get a point across. In some instances this included complete strip searches of the individual and his cell. If the shakedown involved a cell, the inmate would first be strip searched and then required to stand outside his cell while it was searched. The shakedown involved stripping the bunks, checking the mattress, underneath the sink, the shelves for loose pegs where contraband could be stored, etc. Everything was searched including books, towels and especially the toilet. I would like to leave the cell at least decent when finished; however, I would not make the bed. The inmate would then be let back in his cell. If a search occurred when the inmate was at work, in the yard, etc., he would definitely know one was conducted when he returned.

Any inmate at any time and at any place was subject to a shakedown. This was either the "pat" search or "strip" search, depending on the reason for the search. The "pat" search included checking around the collar, back, sides, sleeves, cuffs, under arms, hooked thumb in waist band, across the butt, down each leg, shoes, and slide the hand up into the crotch. In doing a thorough search to prevent contraband from entering the cellhouse, all the inmates coming out of areas like the kitchen or hospital would be searched. I personally, when assigned to the clothing room, would search the crew at noon and at night before they returned to the cellhouse. I never found any major contraband; however, I did find such things as gum and food stuff. I attributed this to the fact that the inmates knew I did thorough searches and shakedowns and realized that it would probably be found.

The inmates who worked on the dock were "shaken down" daily before they started work on the dock and also when they left the dock for any reason including meals and returning to their cells.

The "strip" search was the "mother of all searches." This required the inmates to undress. All items of clothing were thoroughly searched along with their complete body. This included looking in their ears and mouth, making the inmate run his fingers through his hair, looking up his nose with a flashlight, lifting his penis and checking under his balls, checking his arms and hands, spreading his cheeks, and having him lift his feet and wiggle his toes. After the search the inmate was given his clothing back and he dressed. I always thoroughly washed my hands after each search. I never found anything but others did such as hacksaws, blades, handcuff keys, razor blades, and paperclips.

One of the guard's major responsibilities was the enforcement of rules and regulations. To help him numerous metal detectors were located on the island. There was also a portable metal detector which could be taken where needed. Major movements to and from work, the yard, clothing room, dock, and meals were some of the times inmates had to pass through these detectors. It was common for an inmate to try to hide pieces of metal in their shoes. If the detector went off the inmate was searched with a hand device; the item was located, and he would have to again pass through the detector. When I first arrived the inmates had wooden nails in their shoes and wore wooden belt buckles. This was an excellent procedure as it significantly reduced the metal detectors from going off. Later the wood items were replaced with metal items. This was another example of the prison easing policies and procedures.

Inmates who were particularly difficult to handle or would give the guards a rough time, often experienced their own difficulties when passing through metal detectors. The inmate may have had a cigarette pack which contained aluminum foil inside and since they couldn't carry them through as the aluminum foil would set the detector off, they were required to hand the cigarettes to the guard who would also inspect the cigarettes to make sure nothing was concealed therein. Normally the cigarettes would be handed back to the inmate once they proceeded through the metal detector; however, if it was a troublesome inmate, the guard, and I personally did this many times, would lean forward allowing the badge on the hat to discretely set off the metal detector without the inmate knowing what set it off. This was also done even if cigarettes were not involved. Inmates who set off "snitch boxes" were subject to full search and, if the detector went off on their second time through – which we occasionally made sure it did – they were required to completely strip for a full body cavity search. Even the toughest inmate lost much of their dignity while standing in their birthday suit in front of fellow inmates. The rubber glove treatment only made things worse! Normally the inmate wouldn't give the guard guff after that.

There was one inmate who was injured prior to coming to Alcatraz and his injury resulted in a metal plate being inserted in his head. Therefore, every time he went through the detector he would set it off. To ensure he wasn't taking anything, or other inmates weren't planting things on him, every precaution had to be taken to ensure it was only the metal plate in his head that was setting the detector off.

CHAPTER SIXTEEN

Manning the towers was not just demanding, but stressful. It required vigilance and alertness to what was immediately in view and what trouble might be brewing from a broader perspective, especially around the outside perimeter of the prison. There were five towers on Alcatraz all located outside the prison compound. Every three months a roster with shift assignments was made and the guard spent five days a week at that specific shift. Normally, when the roster was changed the guard would get a different tower and hours. However, there were a few guards who liked certain shifts, such as the morning shift, and if they asked they could continue working that shift, but at a different post. Guard duty in the towers was an eight-hour shift, with no lunch relief. You took your lunch with you. The only reading material allowed were post orders. The eyes of the guard were to be trained primarily on those areas under their control and secondarily on surrounding areas. Reporting for duty required a visit to the Captain's office for instructions. The officer on duty in the control center would call or radio the respective tower to alert a guard that his relief was coming and the person soon to be approaching was authorized to do so.

If a guard grew sleepy or just wanted to move about, especially on the morning or evening watch, he would go out on the catwalk that surrounded the tower and pace that small confined area just to stay awake or alert. In later years guards were allowed to possess two-way radios. The option to be in communication with guards in the other towers or the control center relieved some of the boredom. To ensure that guards, particularly those on duty after dark, weren't napping or paying close attention, a shift lieutenant wielding a flashlight, would use a flashing technique, by directing the light beam to the tower. The guard on duty was required to flash back in acknowledgement that he'd seen the lieutenant's signal. One of the lieutenants was "flash happy" and would flash from different locations in a short amount of time, each time expecting recognition, and a flash back. He would visit the tower and socialize for a short period of time. Many times, after leaving, he would immediately go around the yard wall and flash again. Then he would go to another location, wait a few minutes, and do it again. Whenever that particular lieutenant was on duty the guards were extra alert expecting to see numerous flashes. If a guard became ill while on duty and it was necessary to relieve him, the lieutenant would transfer the main gate guard to serve the remainder of the shift.

Accommodations in the towers, except Tower #5, consisted of a stool to sit on, a toilet, and a phone. Tower #5 had no toilet. Each tower guard was issued weapons and ammunition – pistol and carbine. On the road tower (Tower No. 2) and dock tower (Tower No.1) a 30.06 was also available - loaded and ready to use

A lone man, weapons, a bullhorn, accommodations, a flashlight for the night shifts, and an elevated view were the stark reality of guard duty in the towers. The penthouse view, with these luxury accommodations, afforded an outlook on the dock and waterfront. Tower guards had no direct contact with inmates, except the potential for a verbal warning, a warning shot or a shot to kill if an escape attempt or serious incident occurred.

Activity in the water around the island was part of the observation duty. Buoys located 300 yards off the shoreline of Alcatraz surrounded the island. Signs on the island that were visible in daylight also warned against unauthorized approaches to the island. Only prison or Coast Guard boats were allowed to travel beyond the buoys toward the island. Breach of the boundary prompted an initial verbal warning amplified through the use of a bull horn. Failure to comply with the verbal warning resulted in several rifle or pistol shots fired across the bow of the boat. I personally never had reason to fire at a boat, but I know several guards who did.

Tower No. 1 was the only tower consistently manned 24 hours a day during my time at Alcatraz. Known simply as the "Dock Tower," it was raised well above the ground and located on the dock. When a shift change occurred, the relieving guard would walk to the dock and wait outside a locked gate. The guard in the tower would lower a rope with a key attached. The incoming guard used the key to unlock the gate and then lock it after himself. Entrance to the tower was gained through a trap door that the guard inside the tower unlocked. The new duty guard checked weapons and ammunition and reported to the control center that he was in place to begin his shift.

Tower No. 2, known as the "Road Tower," was significant for when it wasn't manned. The tower was elevated above the ground on the side of the island facing San Francisco. Prior to May 6, 1962, the tower was manned 24 hours a day. Effective that date the Bureau of Prisons downgraded the tower to being manned only for the day shift, eliminating the evening and morning watch. This was done due to budgetary constraints. After this date a guard was only on duty from 5:00 A.M. to 6:00 P.M. From this tower the guard could observe the movement of inmates from the prison yard as they proceeded to the industries building for work. Additionally, kitchen yard orderlies were aware and required to stay within view of Tower No. 2 and the guard could easily observe their movement. I once had occasion to cock my gun and use the bullhorn to verbally warn a yard orderly who strayed from the visual boundaries. He promptly returned to view and stood at attention until told to continue his duties. Later he asked me if I would have indeed pulled the trigger and tried to shoot him if he hadn't responded to my command. I replied: "I'm not sure. Try it again and we will see." My response was intentionally ambiguous. They were simply testing me in hopes of calculating what action I might or might not take and that would be one more informational item for those whose favorite pastime was plotting escape strategies. Changing of the guard in Tower No. 2 involved a two-step process. The guard arriving for duty walked around a catwalk and the yard wall to an electronically locked gate. The guard who was being relieved pushed a button inside the tower to open the lock and the new guard would enter. Once inside the tower, the new duty guard confirmed that weapons and ammunition issued were accounted for and then he would radio the control center and report "Two Tower is manned."

An incident occurred which supports the comment that this tower was significant for when it wasn't manned. In December 1962, Tower No 2 was not manned when two inmates, John Paul Scott and Daryl Lee Parker escaped into the water around Alcatraz Island and subsequently were caught. It doesn't take a brain surgeon to figure out that these escapes were timed according to when the tower wouldn't be manned.

Tower No. 3 was located by the water tower and was raised well above the ground. It was manned only when the inmates were working in industries, Monday through Friday - 8 A.M. to 4:30 P.M. On June 11, 1962, in what is one of the most famous incidents of Alcatraz history, brothers John and Clarence Anglin, along with Frank Lee Morris escaped when Tower 3 was not manned – and the inmates knew this. A catwalk led to the industries building and the Tower. It was a long walk, down steep stairs just to get to it. The stairs were half rotten and you had to be very careful going out there. Seagulls perched on the steps and there were nests. They were quick to attack if they perceived your movement up or down the stairs as a threat to their eggs or their young. It was a "heck" of a long and miserable trek.

Tower No. 4, known as the Industry Tower, was located on the roof of the old industries building. It also was manned only during hours when industries were in operation. Tower No. 4 was legendary for one particular foiled escape attempt that occurred during an industries work shift and involved three inmates. Significant to this attempted escape was that the inmates could observe when the tower guard sat down on the toilet in Tower No. 4. On the day of the escape attempt, the inmates waited for the guard to take a toilet break and when he did, they rushed the guard on the industry floor, knocked him out, and tied him up. Then they exited through windows of the industries building that led onto the roof. Their intent was to rush Tower No. 4 and take it over. Nature's call, however, hadn't relieved the guard of his vigilance to duty. He had his rifle in his lap and shot and killed two of the three inmates attempting to escape.

Tower No. 5 was located on the ground by the back of the kitchen and basement. It was manned only from 5 A.M. to 7 P. M. while the inmates were in the kitchen areas either preparing food or eating it. This duty station was actually a cubicle and had no restroom. The guard observed the back of the cellhouse and issued keys to inmates or others who were authorized to go into the clothing room or the kitchen basement. The guard occasionally might see an inmate exit the kitchen long enough to retrieve potatoes or some other supply.

Tower No. 6 was not manned at all while I was on the island and was removed during my time at Alcatraz. It was located on the roof of the main cellhouse. Inmates involved in escape attempts in both June 1962 and December 1962 apparently factored in the absence of this tower. The path used in both celebrated escapes included stealthy steps in view of this absent lookout post.

Guard duty was serious business, but pranks occasionally happened. One favorite of the senior officers was to tell a new guard to call the power house engineer in the middle of the night, usually about 2:00 A.M., and report that the powerhouse was losing steam. When the new guard complied, he'd be on the receiving end of a grumpy lesson from the engineer. In short, losing steam was rarely a problem because there was frequent excess burn-off at the powerhouse.

Kenny on yard wall steps

Vicki (age 2) on parade grounds for ice cream social

Kenny in inmate recreation yard.

Kenny, Vicki, & Cathy in front of Administration Bldg.

Kenny, Vicki, & Cathy in front of Tower 2 (road tower).

Cell with dummy head. June 1962 escape.

Cell where inmate dug out in June 1962.

Jim on a return visit to Alcatraz, west end of Broadway, second tier.

Jim and Cathy at rear door of apt. 108, 64 Bldg.
(our first apartment).

Courtesy San Francisco Chronicle

Jim escorting last chain off Alcatraz, Jim in light colored suit,
Fort Mason dock.

Courtesy San Francisco Chronicle

Jim escorting last chain off Alcatraz, Jim in light colored suit,
Fort Mason dock.

James B. Albright

DATE	Place of Leaving	TIME	Sp'd'mtr reading	Place of Arrival	TIME	Sp'd'mtr reading	Miles trip	total
23	6-21	Alcatraz	5:54 pm	44992	Lovelock Nevada	4:00 pm	45306	314	
24	6-22	Lovelock Nevada	6:00 am	45307	Wendover Nevada	"	45615	308	
25	6-23	Wendover Nevada	"	45616	Rock Springs Wyoming	3:58 pm	45922	306	
26	6-24	Rock Springs Wyoming	"	45923	Denver Colorado	4:00 pm	46265	342	
27	6-25	Denver Colorado	"	46270	Holdredge Nebraska	5:15 pm	46783	513	
28	6-26	Holdredge Nebraska	"	46784	Iowa City Iowa	5:20 pm	47299	515	
29	6-27	Iowa City Iowa	"	47300	Marion Illinois	6:15 pm	47700	400	

Copy of Jim's travel schedule leaving Alcatraz

CHAPTER SEVENTEEN

The presence of usually about 155 inmates and the accessibility of machines, tools, and other objects in the industries operation required a heightened vigilance by guards on duty. Various industry shop areas were located in a new two-story structure that housed the industries operations and was situated outside the main cellhouse and below the recreation yard.

Inmates were given the opportunity to work in the industries or elsewhere in the prison. If they refused, they lost good-time and other privileges and could be put in segregation. Industries work was a way for the inmates to occupy themselves as well as create a source of income. A large number of inmates preferred this type of work. Walking to work from the main cellhouse to the industries building was the furthest an inmate ventured past the walls of the prison. The walk provided the closest view of San Francisco and the bay that an inmate could get. Not to overlook one important fact, he got to breathe fresh outside air.

Industry shops operated 8 A.M. to 4 P.M. Monday through Friday. Oversight of the mass of resourceful inmates was the job of three guards and 10 to 12 shop foremen, who were wage board employees assigned to supervise the industries work done by the inmates. One guard was stationed inside the industries building and patrolled the interior. Another guard was located outside in what was known as the "work area." A lieutenant oversaw the shift and rotated his patrol inside and outside the building.

An old industries building, which was in extremely poor condition, was used for storage during my time on Alcatraz. I imaging there must be many interesting stories about work in that old building. It was now used to store supplies for the industries operations. When these supplies were needed the inmates, under very close supervision by the shop foreman and the outside guard, would retrieve what was needed.

Other personnel affiliated with the prison industries operation included a variety of wage board employees, including a superintendent, assistant superintendent, business manager, assistant business manager, accountant and clerk.

There were several designated work areas located within the industries building, with each specialty performed in a specific location within the building. The tailor operation and clothing factory, along with a brush and broom shop were located on the second floor. The laundry, model shop and shoe-repair shops were on the first floor. Also, on the first floor was a small electric and maintenance shop, where workers performed maintenance and repairs on the machinery that was pivotal to all the operations, including sewing, broom and brush machines. A chief electrician, a civilian wage board employee, managed and supervised the inmates who worked in these areas. The model shop repaired wooden desks, chairs, and other items.

Most of the industry inmates I encountered during my four years appeared to be busy and to a certain extent happy, but I was warned early never to let my guard down. The industries kept men occupied, but the seemingly calm order of the operation could explode in seconds due to the proximity of tools that could become weapons in the hands of an inmate with a score to settle against another inmate or a guard. Metal detectors that prisoners had to pass through after working in industries reduced the temptation to steal items to transform into weapons. Consequently, dirty deeds were often done right in the shops. In fact, three weeks after my industries training, a fight broke out in the glove shop between inmate Beck (AZ 1168) and inmate Baker (AZ 1305). Beck stabbed Baker in the forehead and shoulders with a pair of scissors. Many other incidents occurred during my tenure but this was the most serious.

In February 1961, a homemade bar spreader was found in the brush shop. It was made from a piece of pipe, threaded bolt and a piece of "C" clamp. It had to be made during working hours in the shop. We never discovered who made this spreader nor how he intended to get it to his cell, but I feel he probably intended to try to smuggle it in via the laundry hampers. These hampers contained inmate clothing and were processed and cleared at the dock before being delivered to the cellhouse. I often wondered how the inmate could have made this spreader while under close supervision, how long it took him to make it, what other instruments of destruction did he make, and did he ever get any of them up to his cell. We will never know.

Sometimes a joke would be pulled on one of the guards. Officer Kenny Blair had an inmate, Lucky Juelick (AZ 1190), play a prank on me. I was outside the industries building, new to the job, and my assignment was to keep a check on the industries officer, Officer Blair, who was outside the new industries building with 2 or 3 inmates getting supplies. My job was to physically see him every 15 minutes. Well, 15 minutes to me meant 15 minutes, so the time is approaching and I have not seen Officer Blair. Fifteen minutes arrives and passes, 16 minutes, 17 minutes – I started to worry and was about to take some action. About that time inmate Lucky Juelick popped his head out the door and said "Mr. Blair said to tell you he can't see you. He is all tied up." Before I could react, Officer Blair popped his head out and said: "Here I am." He put inmate Juelick up to that. During a recent visit to Alcatraz I was on the same boat with Lucky Juelick and I reminded him of this incident. We both had a laugh.

Most of the Alcatraz industry shops generated positive revenues for what was then known as the Federal Prison Industry (F.P.I.). The military was the best customer of the F.P.I. shops. Contract work for the military provided comfortable profit margins to them.

The clothing factory was a huge resource for the industries operation. For example, in April 1962, the clothing factory received an order for 24,000 pairs of hospitals trousers to be used at a nearby Veteran's Administration (VA) Hospital. The military and armed forces were other major clients for industries goods and all the industries areas produced items used at Alcatraz.

The main industry on the island was the laundry, but this produced lower revenues because of the cost to transport, by barge, fresh water from the mainland to the island. Contracts with the military and a Veteran's Administration Hospital resulted in shipment of mass bundles of laundry to be cleaned at Alcatraz. When laundry shipments arrived, the clothing was unloaded from the barge. A thorough search of incoming bundles, involving the use of a "spectroscope" that enabled a guard to scan for alien objects was conducted and then the bundles were transported to the laundry facility. Clothing was laundered, dried, folded, and placed in bags and then taken to the dock where another search occurred before it was loaded on a barge for transport to the client. The laundry did not go without incident. Once when I was operating the spectroscope a crowbar showed up in one of the duffel bags with the dirty laundry. Also, before my time, an escape attempt involved an inmate who worked on the dock. He stole a military uniform and used it in his escape attempt.

Another interesting incident involved Officer "Cowboy Jack" Shepler. He was a guard and a little bit crazy. I believe he got the nickname "cowboy" from the inmates who worked on the dock. How they came up with that I guess was because he was a little wild, like a cowboy. Anyway, Cowboy Jack worked on the dock and had 5 inmates working for him. When the barge came in the inmates would unload the many bundles of military laundry to be sent to the industries (laundry) for cleaning, and run them through the spectroscope. Well, Cowboy Jack was outside on the dock and Lieutenant Double Tough Ordway was inside monitoring the spectroscope. Cowboy Jack got a couple of inmates who were working on the dock to open one of the laundry bags and Cowboy Jack crawled inside. I can't imagine what the inmates thought, but he had them close the laundry bag and put it through the spectroscope. Well here is Lieutenant Double Tough Ordway, in the spectroscope room watching the bags of laundry go through. Suddenly he came running out yelling "escape attempt, escape attempt." Needless to say he wasn't at all happy when he discovered the joke that Cowboy Jack played. I am sure Lieutenant Ordway wrote a rather harsh comment on Cowboy Jack's performance card concerning the incident.

Furniture produced for military use in the first half of the 20th century was wood, and the prison industries at Alcatraz for many years operated a financially successful furniture refinishing shop. In the late 1950s and early 1960s, prison industries began investigating what its role might be in metal furniture assembly for military installations. Contracts, such as one with Hamilton Air Force Base, for work done by inmates in the furniture refinishing shop were moving to completion.

In an October 1959 monthly status report on Alcatraz prison industries, Warden Paul Madigan communicated the following to the Director of the Federal Bureau of Prisons:

"Industries are going ahead with the construction of the new clothing factory located in the old laundry area. The painting and general construction is completed. The cutting table is made and in place and we are now awaiting the materials from Los Angeles to install the overhead electrical lines. We have plenty of work in this factory since we are now working on orders of 87,000 cooks and bakers pants for the QM Corps. We still have enough work in the furniture factory to keep 21 men occupied; however, it will not be too many months until we run out of wood, desks and chairs. Most of the offices in the Army and Navy and other government agencies are turning to metal furniture which we have not attempted to finish at this institution. Hamilton AFB and Camp Mather, near Sacramento, have furnished us with 100 desks to

be refinished and we have done work on two desks for Fort Miley to give them a sample of our work. We may be able to get further work from this source in the near future.

We have 35 inmates employed in the glove factory and we probably have more difficulty in this particular unit than any other shop. The entire shop is congested and we recently had 2300 welders gloves returned because the fingers were crooked and poorly formed, This work will have to be corrected without cost which will cause some resentment in the shop, however, we have continued to get along without any serious trouble in this area even through there was considerable bickering about the group pay scale when it was originally installed. When we get into our new quarters and more room is available I feel that this shop should run much more smoothly. Mr. Duncan from industries was here between September 9th and 18th helping us establish the Quality Inspection Control Program.

The brush shop continues to operate efficiently and is now working on Navy orders. This is probably the best shop in the industries since we have a strong officer in charge, Mr. Christopherson, who knows everything that the inmates think and do."

CHAPTER EIGHTEEN

Playgrounds normally are nice places to go and have fun and for the most part that was what the recreation yard at Alcatraz was all about –relaxing, games, outside, fresh air, and a good view. From the yard the Golden Gate Bridge was visible and the surrounding bay area could be seen from the top of the yard steps. A nice place for a tea party! However, it was also one of the most dangerous areas at Alcatraz because of the potential for assaults and sudden eruption of fights and arguments among the inmates. I was told shortly after my arrival that it had the reputation as a potentially dangerous area and that a guard had to always stay alert and be quick to act on even the smallest of incidents as they could easily result in large-scale fights or disruptions.

On weekends and holidays, the recreation yard was the one place, in addition to the dining room, where as many as 150 to 200 inmates might be together at one time. However, it was rare for all the inmates to be in the yard at the same time. Typically some were in isolation, some were on kitchen duty, and occasionally some were running scared of their vulnerability to other inmates in the yard and simply didn't want to go into that setting. Inmates could spend up to a total of five hours per day, only on weekends, in the recreation yard. Like all other activities, recreation yard time was a privilege and could be withheld. Inmates who worked seven days a week in the kitchen earned their privilege of exercise and yard time on weekdays.

There were small folding chairs and tables in the yard for the inmates to use for cards, dominoes, and board games. Popular activities included checkers, chess and backgammon. Inmates also played shuffleboard and basketball. Some would use the yard space for running or walking. Handball was a big favorite and two courts were available. Inmates could buy their own handballs and gloves. Softball was also played with over the wall being out. When hit over the wall the ball would normally go down the industries building roof and the inmates would have to wait until someone issued them another ball for their game to resume.

Some inmates used the weightlifting equipment that was available in the yard. They could check out the free weights and had to check them in when finished. I remember one prisoner who took his body conditioning seriously and frequently was seen lifting weights. One day in the yard I saw him get down on his stomach and reach out with his arms. He them pushed down with his hands and pulled his body upright into a handstand. That wasn't too impressive; however, he then walked across the yard, up the steps, through the metal detector, into the cellhouse, and up the steps to his cell – all on his hands. Now that was impressive! The strength and endurance that he communicated with this unusual feat did not go unnoticed by the other inmates or the guards. In the yard the inmates sat and talked, played games, exercised and probably even plotted for Lord knows what. In their cells they were alone, but here they mingled. Fights, assaults, and other disturbances occurred swiftly and unexpectantly.

Unarmed guards were assigned to the yard and patrolled the area on foot, always being vigilant of their surroundings and the potential dangers that lurked. Three armed guards were stationed on a catwalk, elevated about 25 feet above the yard. The catwalk surrounded the yard. If a guard observed a disturbance or outbreak, rule number one was to blow his whistle, thus alerting both the other guards and the other inmates. Most of the inmates in the area could see what was going on and would back away so as not to be perceived to be involved. Guards quickly assessed the disruptive scenario to determine if it might be a ruse designed to conceal a more serious or large-scale situation. If it involved two inmates, the unarmed guards in the yard would step-in and quickly break it up. But if it appeared that an inmate had a weapon of some sort, a guard on the yard wall would shout a warning. If order wasn't immediately restored, he would normally fire a warning shot from his rifle. The guard, at his discretion, was authorized to fire a hit. Stabbing wounds weren't common but did happen. I recall one fight in the yard where an inmate had a knife. After using the weapon on an inmate, he passes it to another inmate, presumably for hiding or disposal. Inmates involved in fights, etc., would immediately be escorted to segregation and the lieutenant would conduct an investigation. Of course, when questioned, the inmates all adhered to their strict "Code of Silence."

Recreation yard guard duty could be tense. But some moments and events earned legendary status among the guards for other reasons. One such instance was a particular sequence of events experienced by a guard whose bad day got worse. A fight broke out between two inmates and the guard stationed on wall number one grabbed his whistle but failed to get the sound to come out to alert the yard officers and inmates about the fight as his teeth fell out. When he grabbed his carbine to fire a warning shot, his gun jammed. To top it off he then attempted to draw his pistol, but it caught in the holster. Finally, he declared "Screw it, Let them fight,"

There were several inmates that other inmates looked up to and they were quite powerful. They could get just about anything they wanted or something done, of course for a price. Their power was reflected by how high on the steps they sat. Bumpy Johnson was one inmate who sat on the top step.

When the recreational day started the inmates were required to first proceed through a metal detector before entering the yard, and when the day was over they had to pass through the metal detector before returning to the main cellhouse. I often wondered, how did they ever get metal items through the detector, as we all knew they used them in the yard on occasions?

CHAPTER NINETEEN

The "dock" was one area that was extremely busy as all people coming to or leaving Alcatraz, for any reason, had to go to and from the island by way of the island boat, the "Warden Johnston." The Warden Johnston, named after the first warden at Alcatraz, was very small and not equipped with modern radar. This made some crossings, particularly on real foggy days, quite treacherous. I was told the boat was condemned for 13 years. A boat schedule was published and made available to all island residents. Approximately 12 – 16 times each day the Warden Johnston could be seen leaving for Fort Mason and returning to Alcatraz. The "Alcatraz Navy" actually had two boats assigned to its fleet; however, the other boat, the "Warden Madigan" was available only for emergencies.

A boat Operator, a wage board employee, was assigned as the boat operator. He was the Captain of the boat and was responsible for its operation. A guard, the "Boat Officer," assisted him and whenever the boat left or returned the boat operator and boat officer were aboard. On November 13, 1961, Warden O.G. Blackwell sent a memorandum to all employees concerning the boat operations. It stated:

"Effective immediately, certain changes in methods of boat operation are in effect and any instructions to the contrary that have been listed before should be disregarded and destroyed.

1. *To permit an orderly boarding of the boat and to prevent long waits in the waiting room, passengers may board the boat any time after the "ten-minute" whistle has blown. To make this a safe procedure, the boat operator should be sure that his boat is ready for boarding and that the boat officer is available to assist anyone who might need help in boarding safely before sounding the whistle.*

2. *The present procedure for children on their way to and from school will continue to be followed. (When parents are aboard with school children, it would be most helpful if they would assist in their supervision).*

3. *Common courtesy dictates that gentlemen will step aside and permit ladies and children to board first, or, in some cases, assist them in boarding. Gentlemen accompanied by their families may board the boat with them, making it possible for them to assist with packages and the safety of their family members. Disembarking will be carried out in the same manner.*

4. *Parents accompanied by children will arrange to keep them under their supervision and insure orderly conduct while on the boat.*

5. *Unfortunately, we still have some who insist on disregarding existing regulations, TO REMAIN SEATED UNTIL THE DISEMBARK WHISTLE HAS BLOWN. This practice creates considerable hazard for the boat officer and operator in trying to tie up the boat and fasten the gangplank. It is*

> *also a very dangerous practice for the individual and could very well result in the loss of life or serious injury. All boat operators and all boat officers are expected to report to the Warden or Associate Warden any further failure to comply with this reasonable safety practice.*
>
> 6. *It should be remembered by all concerned that the boat operator is responsible for the safe operation of his boat, therefore, he is in COMPLETE CHARGE and his decisions and orders are final while embarking, disembarking, or under way."*

The day watch boat officer was assigned an 8 hour shift 7 days a week - 8:00 A.M. to 4:30 P.M. – and his responsibilities included assisting people on and off the boat, helping carry groceries and mail if needed, escorting visitors through the metal detector and to the dock office to sign in, helping watch inmates working on the dock, and helping search inmates going to and from work. When the boat pulled into the dock he was responsible for locking the boat and when ready to depart to Fort Mason unlock it. To lock and unlock the boat, the guard would get the key from the guard in Tower No. 1 and return it when completed. The key was raised and lowered by use of a rope. Counting passengers getting on/off the boat and reporting this to the control center in case of an emergency was also his duty. At one time the guard had to check everybody's name on the boat list. Early on when I didn't know most people's names, let alone the children, and since everyone had to be listed, it took time. I would pick a teenager and ask that person to tell me who the kids were. This person would name them and I'd check them off. It didn't take me long to know everyone and this became easier and quicker. Inmates traveled on the same boat as everyone else. Sometimes 4 or 5 could be on the boat at one time. They usually sat back on the fantail. All had leg irons, belly chains and handcuffs. They, of course were escorted, and entered and exited last. Inmates were not allowed to travel on the same bus with other passengers. They would hold the inmates on the boat until the bus left. The inmates would then be escorted off the boat, go through the metal detector, and when the bus returned they were taken to the prison for processing.

On one occasion the boat was being tied up at Fort Mason between piers 3 and 4. As the boat came in, the boat officer, Dick Waszak, reached down with the grappling hook to grab the rope and secure the boat. This time when reaching down he slipped and fell in. He went under the boat and came up on the other side of the dock and could easily have been crushed.

One night going across it was quite foggy and hard to see. Being the boat officer I was out on the bow watching, as the boat had no radar. All of a sudden I heard a horn and looked up. There was this big freighter coming right at us. I yelled to the boat operator and he hit reverse, spun the wheel and backed away.

Security procedures actually started before the boat docked. Security was very tight and strict on the dock but even more so whenever the island boat was nearing Alcatraz. This was because inmates worked on the dock during the day – Monday through Friday only, performing many tasks including unloading items and handling furniture, etc. These inmates were considered trustees and were highly recommended, normally by the Captain or a Lieutenant. The warden or assistant warden approved all inmates assigned to work on the dock. A memorandum dated January 4, 1960, addressed to the captain, signed by the Associate Warden O.G. Blackwell, assigned inmate Robinson (AZ 1151) to the dock crew. It read "Effective December 31, 1959 the above named inmate was assigned to the Dock Crew. The Record Office will furnish photographs of the inmate to all regularly manned Towers and to the Dock Lieutenant."

Inmates assigned to the dock normally were very well behaved; however, they would sometimes push the button to see how far they could get. Early in my training when I was assigned to the dock, I was smoking a cigar. One of the inmates came up to me and said "Oh, boss, that cigar sure smells good." What he was doing was hinting for a cigar without asking because he can't ask anybody for anything. He later stated "I am not asking for one." I said "No, I would give you hell if you ever looked like you were." I am sure he was testing me as a new guard. Asking a guard for something could get an inmate in segregation; however, most of the time you would tell them they knew better and do nothing. If you ever gave them anything your job could also be in jeopardy and even worse would be the fact that they now had you in a position where they could use that as a form of "blackmail" and you didn't want to be in that position. Next time they might ask for something more serious, like drugs, etc. I had several incidents early during my training where inmates would hint about cigars or cigarettes. Apparently word got out not to and shortly thereafter they ceased asking me. I often wondered what value a cigar would have in the prison as they were not allowed, only cigarettes and tobacco.

The strict security for the inmates started whenever the boat was drawing near the Alcatraz dock. In clear view of the guard in Tower No. 1 was a painted white line located by the garage on the dock. When the boat was approaching the island the boat officer would inform the control center, by radio that they were nearing the dock. The control center would inform the Lieutenant on the dock that the boat was approaching and a whistle would blow alerting the inmates to immediately line up behind the white line. There were 5 inmates working on the dock and they were also verbally told "OK, 5 on the line the boat is approaching." Most of the time the inmates knew it was approaching and would go to the line before the whistle or being told. Occasionally, especially for a new guard, they may wait to be told. Once on the line the officer in Tower No. 1 would inform the control center, by radio, saying "got 5 on the line." The control center would give clearance to the boat to dock. After unloading the boat, the officer would lock the boat to the dock. Visitors coming to the island for any reason were required to go through the metal detector and sign in at the dock office. After that they would be taken to wherever they were going. Once the last civilian left the dock the tower officer would give the OK and the inmates would be released off the line to resume work.

Not to over look an important fact, there were 2 or 3 other people who worked on the docks during the day time when the inmates were present. These were civilian personnel (mechanics, mechanical services men for crane and forklift) and the Lieutenant. When the boat officer was gone for the 30 minute round trip to and from the island, a non-guard would be watching the inmates. Everybody, no matter what their job, had one major duty and that was the care, custody and security of the inmates. They really were guards first.

When the boat officer wasn't involved with the boat trips, he had other duties to perform. Basically, he reported to the Lieutenant on the dock and did whatever was required, normally working on the dock. One thing he also did was drive the bus. When an island resident was going to leave on the boat they would walk to the dock (around building 64) or if they needed a ride the bus was sent to get them. Normally, island residents took the bus almost every time after embarking from the boat and the boat officer would drive them to their quarters. The residents could walk to their quarters and some did. The bus trip would leave the dock area, go through the tunnel and "over the top," past the warden's and MTA's quarters, by the entrance to the administrative building and finally down a driveway to the quarters and parade ground.

Twice a week a barge with drinking water and supplies from San Francisco came to the island. There were two large pumps with diesel motors located at the dock and they were used to pump the water from the barge. The barge would come right up beside the dock, hook the water hoses from the island to the barge and pump the water to the island power house, where in turn, it would be pumped to the water tower and the two underground water tanks located by the power house. It took about 24 hours to pump water from the barge to the island locations. On top of the barge was a small fenced in area where any furniture, kitchen supplies, or other supplies for the island were stored for delivery. The supplies, etc., would be unloaded and put on the dock for pick-up. A crane with rope slings was used for unloading, and a forklift on the dock, placed the items onto a truck to be delivered to the various island locations. Inmates usually hooked the hoses up to the barge and unloaded the supplies; however, mechanical services were responsible for the unloading and they had a person assigned to supervise the work.

Other duties and responsibilities of the guard assigned to the Dock and Patrol/Boat Officer, included the evening watch (4:00 P.M. to midnight) and the morning watch (midnight to 8:00 A.M.). There was less activity on the dock during these shifts and no inmates to supervise. They only had scheduled boat runs to contend with. Therefore, in between the boat runs, the guard would patrol the island including the shops, power house, apartments, and East beach, especially during darkness. On the Morning watch the guard was also assigned areas to search. These included the industries, shoe shop, broom and brush shop, clothing factory, laundry, and east beach area, looking for contraband or anything suspicious. I had outside patrol one evening and it was very foggy and damp with cold winds to the point of being scary. There were frequent occasions of it being foggy, damp and cold; however, this one particular evening was a lot more severe. I couldn't see the gate lock to unlock it. I held the flashlight up to find the key hole and by the time I got it located the fog horn went off and I jumped six feet. It scared me to death. You see all kind of things in the thick fog. During the day there are more people, not much of a problem.

Also, there are heavy rains that occur. I was on the midnight to 8 A.M. shift; it was about 2 A.M. and I was making a shakedown of the industries building. All of a sudden a loud booming noise broke the silence. I said to myself: "What the hell is that?" I called the control center and Ralph Burros was on duty. He said "What's up Jim." I said "When it rains real hard does it loosen the rocks and they fall against the building." After he laughed he replied "Scares the hell out of you doesn't it."

While working the evening shift, the officer in the Dock Tower ran out of cigarettes and asked me to give him a pack. This was accomplished by him lowering a rope down from the tower and me attaching the cigarettes to the rope. It was the same procedure and rope that the tower used daily to lower and return the key to the boat's ignition. I planned to stop by my apartment for another pack of cigarettes when the sequence of events suddenly changed. On September 20, 1961, at approximately 9:30 P.M., while walking by the East Beach I shined my flashlight and saw a body floating in the water with nothing on but his jockey shorts. I immediately went to a phone and dialed the "three deuces (222)" which was the emergency phone number to the Control Center. The main gate guard went to get a gaff and arrived at the waters edge accompanied by the Lieutenant. They tried to grab the body by the elastic band of his jockey shorts; however, the waist band tore and they had to stab him in the stomach to bring him in as he was obviously dead and in extremely poor shape. It appeared that he must have served as a feeding for the ocean life. During this ordeal I was thankful I was given the task of moving the "Warden Johnston" out of its slip so the Coast Guard boat could dock there for pick-up of the body. It was later I learned the victim had committed suicide by jumping off the Golden Bridge. I thought there must be an easier way to get to Alcatraz.

One night I was the Dock and Patrol guard and as I came by Tower #1 making my rounds I heard someone yelling "Jim, Jim get my bullets for me." I went over and got closer to the tower and the guard is yelling "I dropped my bullets and they are underneath the tower." I was down on my knees with a flashlight picking up bullets. He was messing with the gun, opened it and the bullets fell out.

Another responsibility included driving the island's pick-up. There was a pick-up and a 2 ½ ton truck for use to haul supplies, food to the kitchen, etc. The officer would drive the truck up and unload the items for the clothing or kitchen. He would get the keys from the Guard on 5 Tower to unlock the grille door. He would hand it to you through a hole in the fence. There was a solid steel door inside and he would have to take the key back after he unlocked the grille door and get the key for the solid steel door. He would open that, put the items in, close it and lock it back up, and return the key to the guard. The kitchen personnel could get the items from inside but were unable to go outside. An incident involving the pickup truck occurred when Officer Joe Martin, wrecked the pickup driving from the dock to various locations with supplies. After coming through the tunnel the road splits with one lane going down to the store and the other going up to the top. Where the road split there was a concrete barrier and Joe drove straight into the barrier damaging the bumper, radiator and grill. That's not an uncommon occurrence, having an accident. Now the rest of the story - He walked back down and Lieutenant Ordway asked him "Where is the truck?" Officer Martin replied "It is on top the hill. I wrecked it. I hit that concrete." Lieutenant Ordway said "What the hell happened?" and Officer Martin said "I told you I don't know how to drive." He didn't. Officer Martin lived down the coast from San Francisco and took the bus back and forth. He also lived in bachelor quarters on Alcatraz five days a week and went home on his days off. The fender on the bus was frequently bent and constantly being repaired. The reason for this was the bus had to go uphill/downhill, around sharp curves, and there were barriers in various locations – easy to hit. The fender got bent so many times that the garage person, Peterson, asked for a rubber fender, which he did not get.

The island had a Volunteer Fire Crew, which I was a member. The fire truck was parked facing down on the left side of the tunnel. It was parked there to not only protect it from the weather but also in case it wouldn't start we could coast it down the hill and get it started. The Dock and Patrol/Boat Officer would run the truck weekly to keep it operational and to make sure everything worked, including the hoses. It never had to be used while I was there. There were small fires when inmates would burn something in their cells, etc., and fire extinguishers were all that was needed. Water hoses were located in the cell blocks. The only time I saw them used was in the cellhouse, but it was not for a fire, but rather the inmates in segregation were acting up and water was used to squelch the uprising. Contrary to stories about guards using fire hoses for the inmates to shower was not correct.

CHAPTER TWENTY

The control center was one of the most interesting and challenging assignments. I personally enjoyed and looked forward to this duty. It was the nerve center of Alcatraz; and the most responsible, busy and demanding, yet rewarding assignment on the island. When I was in training and between shifts, I would watch the control center guard perform his duties, especially operating the controls. Several weeks after having the opportunity to observe the operations of the position, I was assigned to the control center. It was stimulating and I felt a sense of control. The control center was responsible for accountability of all the guns, keys, ammunition, etc., and every time a guard was relieved, a complete inventory was taken. This normally took around 35 minutes. Only a few guards were qualified to be assigned this duty. Whenever an incident happened at Alcatraz, the control center guard was actively involved. The night that Parker-Scott (December 16, 1962) attempted to escape, I was in the control center and the activity was fast and furious.

Every night the officer in the control center was required to enter any unusual activity into a log and sign his name. Routinely I would write, "All OK on the night shift," skip a few lines and sign my name early to ensure I wouldn't forget. During the Parker-Scott break in 1962, I learned my lesson not to do this.

A new control center became operational on August 14, 1961. It contained the armory, lock shop, telephone, boat radio, intercom to the towers, controls for the Salley Port gate, and a red emergency phone. The old control center contained basically the same things, but wasn't as modernized. When the switchboard phone rang it would light up letting the officer know where the call originated. During my training at other posts I was taught that if in trouble to knock a receiver off the hook, it would sound an alarm in the control center. Also, if at any time an emergency arose, the guard on that post was required to dial the "three deuces – 222" on the telephone which rang on the red emergency phone in the control center. The control center guard was then responsible for proper notification and, if necessary, set off the appropriate alarm.

Orders in the Control Center were strict and included not allowing any unauthorized persons out the front gate regardless of who they were. This would include the Warden. If he were taken hostage and was telling me to open the gate, I would not do it. Once when I was on duty in the control center, the Warden and Lieutenant Wier visited me. Lieutenant Wier asked me "Jim what would you do if someone tried to get out of this gate. I replied "I have no idea what I'd do." I then said "I know they are not allowed out the gate and at the time that it is happening, my reaction is going to tell me what to do. But I'll tell you one thing they are not coming out through me because I have a wife and kids down over the hill and they aren't getting near them." The Warden said "That is all I wanted to hear." They left.

At about 9 or 10 P.M. one New Years Eve, I was on duty in the control center. A listening device located in the control center allowed the guard to listen anywhere throughout the cellhouse. Through this device the guard is able to hear just about anything. Well, it was rather quiet and I had turned the speaker up to full volume in the east end – "Seedy Avenue." A loud bang was heard and it startled the hell out of me. An inmate threw a bomb made from match heads onto the main floor and it went off. We never did find out who did it. Again, the inmates instituted their "Code of Silence."

Key chits were used to control the issuing of weapons, etc., and were issued and returned to the Control Center. These chits were round in shape, like a fifty cent coin, and contained the name of the guard. Each guard was issued six to ten of these chits. Similar chits are issued at other institutions but may take different shapes and sizes. A guard could get as many chits as he needed. I personally had six. They were used for control purposes of keys, guns, etc. If I was going to work on a tower for example, I would go to the control center and ask for T2 which would be the keys to Tower No. 2. I would give the control center guard one of my chits and he would put it on the ring for that key and give me in return the chit of the person who has that key – the person I was relieving. I would do the same for any weapons or the gas gun, and ammunition. Then I would go out and take the chits I got of the person I was relieving and I would make sure that I received the keys, any weapons or gas gun, and ammunition from that person. Once I had these items and they were correctly accounted for then I would give him his chits. From that time onward I was responsible for these items until I either returned the items to the control center or I was relieved and got my chits from that person.

Located by the Control Center was the main gate. This position was manned seven days a week, 24 hours a day. The main gate officer was also a person responsible for letting anyone in and out of the cellhouse. During the midnight to 8:00 A.M. and 4:00 P.M. to midnight shift the guard would patrol upper areas of the prison, making 3 to 4 rounds each shift. Rounds included the cellhouse; yard wall; Tower No. 2 where he was required to go inside; Tower No. 5; the kitchen, clothing room and basement; administration building; Warden's and MTA's quarters; and the light house. One of his duties was to check the lights on the outside buildings. Whenever lights were burnt-out he would note this on a "Burned-Out Lights" report which had diagrams of the 50 lights that surrounded the buildings. These forms were turned in to the mechanical department who was responsible for replacing the burnt out light the next day. Reading and censoring books and mail that came to and left the prison was also part of his responsibilities.

A guard position, the "Cellhouse East End," located next to the main gate oversaw inmate visitors and monitored inmate movements to and from their cells if they were needed for work duty.

People throughout the world were curious and fascinated with the mystique of Alcatraz and many wanted to visit. Not all were allowed. This was a maximum security prison, strictly controlled, and not a side show; although I sometimes wondered. Visitors included officials and dignitaries from various countries throughout the world as well as from the United States. They were lured for many reasons, including the tough reputation and history of Alcatraz. Many wanted to see first hand the formidable walls of this seemingly escape proof prison, the alleged torture chambers and the general prison operations. Others visited for official or personal reasons, such as lawyers, priests, etc. All visitors required prior written authorization from the Warden. I do not know all of the reasons or why some visitors were approved and others not, or who requested visits, but I do know that approval by the Warden was not automatic. When the approved visitors arrived and their authorization confirmed they were allowed to board the Warden Johnston at Fort Mason for the trip to the island. I often wondered what went through their minds as they crossed this short but treacherous body of water for the first time, and what their expectations were when they started this journey to visit Alcatraz. Were they excited? Were they tense and scared? Sometimes approval would be granted for 6 visitors and when they arrived a much larger number would be present. This complicated the process, but after getting clearance they normally were allowed to visit. All visitors, for any reason, once they arrived at the dock on Alcatraz went through a metal detector and were required to sign in at the dock office. From there, depending on the purpose of the visit, they would normally be transported to the administrative building for a briefing. Once the briefing was completed, the visitors would be given an escorted tour. There were strict limits on where and what they could see and no one was allowed to go on their own. Some, but very few, were allowed to talk to the inmates.

I personally did not get directly involved with most of the visitors; however, occasionally I would be on duty when they arrived and were given the tour.

Various levels of visitors and foreign officials/dignitaries from many countries in the world visited Alcatraz. They came from England, Morocco, Argentina, Soviet Union, Libya, Australia, Iraq, Indonesia, Bolivia, Egypt, Iran, Brazil, Korea, Thailand, Japan, Greece, Poland – to name only a few – to witness first hand what this prison – Alcatraz – was all about. It fascinated so many and for different reasons. I often wondered: What do these individuals tell others after they returned to their homes? What were their impressions? Did the prison meet their expectations?

Local visitors from Government and Law Enforcement Agencies, Congress, judges, Bureau of Prisons, Department of Justice, police, lawyers, press, etc., were the most frequent to visit. Their visits were for a variety of reasons, mostly official.

Ball teams and other celebrities were also authorized. Inmates were big sports fans and they knew if they got into trouble and a ball team came through they might not be able to talk to the players or even see them. The ball teams could visit the cellhouse but couldn't visit segregation or the hospital. I was working the main gate when a sports group came through. I got an autograph from Warren Spahn and Stan "The Man" Musial. In August 1961, five members of the Milwaukee Brewers baseball team visited and chatted with some of the inmates. A big attraction for the inmates was when boxing great "Jersey Joe Walcott" visited. He was allowed to talk with the inmates and those who enjoyed boxing really received him well.

The inmates loved getting personal visitors; normally limited to family members, priests, etc., and the freedom from their cells that came along with getting a visitor. However, inmate visitation was not automatic, but was a privilege that had to be earned. Also, inmate visitors had to be pre-approved and receive permission to board the boat at Pier 4, Fort Mason. Once on the island they went through a metal detector, registered at the dock office, and were driven by bus to the entrance of the administration building. They were escorted at all times. From there they went to one of the four visitor stations located adjacent to the main gate at the edge of the main cellhouse. The inmate and visitor could view each other through a glass partition. Speaker phones, with buttons to push and talk, were available to communicate. A guard would monitor the conversation. I was surprised that there were not that many inmate visitations. Inmates could be granted one visit per month with each visit lasting up to two hours. Privileges, including visiting rights could be lost if an inmate's conduct during the visit was inappropriate.

Visitors to island residents were also allowed. Approval had to be obtained in advance and the visitor was either met at Fort Mason by the resident or met when the boat docked at Alcatraz. The boat officer was notified in advance. The visitor also went through a metal detector and registered at the dock office. Visitors to island residents were not allowed to visit inside the cellhouse and access was limited to island facilities, i.e., parade ground or apartment.

CHAPTER TWENTY-ONE

In early June 1962, I went with a pick-up softball team from Alcatraz to play a friendly game with a team from San Francisco. I was chasing a fly ball when I stepped in a gopher hole and twisted my knee. It continued to hurt and I went to a local hospital to have it examined. It wasn't broken but severely sprained and serious enough that they wrapped it and had me on crutches. This didn't really interfere with my duties as a guard, because at that time I was assigned to the clothing room and extensive movement wasn't necessary. Further, I expected to be off the crutches in a short period of time.

On the morning of June 12, 1962, I was still in bed as my shift started at 9:00 A.M. that morning. The emergency alarm in the prison sounded and it startled me. It was loud enough for all island residents to hear and I'd never heard that before. The clock said 7:10 A.M. as I quickly collected my thoughts, got dressed and headed for the prison. There was no question of what I had to do. When an employee, whether on or off duty, hears the emergency alarm they are to report to the prison with haste. What a time for an emergency I thought, with me on crutches. About halfway up the hill I met the Lieutenant and asked him "What's up?" He replied "I don't know. We have a couple of missing inmates." He told me to go watch the back of the cellhouse, which I immediately did. Small pieces of information slowly filtered in and when my lunch relief arrived curiosity was killing me. I desperately wanted to know what happened and see what was going on first-hand. By this time I knew which inmates were missing and went directly to the cell of one of them – John Anglin. As I stepped up to his cell I could see the false head still in place on his bunk. I was amazed how real it looked. I also knew that when the alarm sounded the Warden and Captain had already implemented the escape plan and wheels were in motion to locate them. The missing were John Anglin (AZ 1476), his brother Clarence Anglin (AZ 1485) and Frank Lee Morris (AZ 1441). I recalled that in all prior attempts, I think there were about 13 of them, no one had ever escaped; many tried, but all were accounted for one way or another and I honestly thought the same thing would happen here. I thought, the fact that many tried and none made it, and all the inmates were fully aware of this - "Why would they take the risk?" Stories concerning the escapee's whereabouts were all over the map, but the bottom line was they still had not been located. In the meantime I wanted to learn more about how the escape evolved, and traced the route they took from the cell to the water. This opened my eyes, and reality set in. The prison staff, from the warden on down, gave them all the opportunities they needed to make it happen. Not to undercut their brilliant scheming and planning, they also took advantage of poor management and other factors that aided their plan. When authorities finally decided that they couldn't locate the inmates they officially listed them as missing, presumed dead (drowned). In a July 1962, report from Warden Blackwell to the Director of Prisons, Blackwell wrote "with the exception of the negligence on the part of the staff permitting such an escape to be possible, all employees in each and every department willingly and without complaint worked long and unusual hours attempting to secure the institution and to find the three escapees or, if possible, their floating bodies in the bay." What actually occurred as I know it, heard about it, or made an intelligent judgment about it, made me realize that I too was a part of all this. The story will have no ending until all three are accounted for one way or another; however, what actually occurred I want to explain, good and bad.

All the control, the restrictions, the strict regulations, the constant monitoring of inmate movement couldn't stop these three inmates from planning and executing this most ingenious and famous escape. They did escape and that was bad enough, but how they did it is most interesting. This famous escape was glamorized in the movie "Escape from Alcatraz" starring Clint Eastwood. What is the hard pill to swallow is that it all started with blankets!

Frank Morris, the Anglin Brothers and Allen West plotted the perfect escape for many months. Morris, worked in the library, was extremely intelligent and was probably the mastermind of the plan. West (AZ 1335) was the inmate credited with discovering the escape route. John Anglin worked for me in the clothing room and his brother Clarence worked in the barber shop, which was crucial to their plan.

The top of B-Block was quite dirty and the bars needed painting – from the top of B-Block to the ceiling was nothing but the bars and you could see through them. A decision was made to clean and paint this area and inmate Allen West (AZ 1335) was assigned to perform that task and no guard was assigned to look after him. I was really surprised by the fact that he wasn't being supervised. West noticed an air vent that led to the roof was directly above where he was assigned to work. He also noticed the poor condition of the area, and I feel that it was at this point that he saw a way out. He thought if he could some how come out of his cell, enter the utility corridor and climb up he could escape through the vent. However, stumbling blocks confronted him; getting out of his cell and into the utility corridor; the vent was secured with bars and they would have to be cut or bent; and the outside air vent itself had to be removed.

West got with Morris and the Anglin Brothers and discussed what he found. A plan was devised and the decision was reached to go forward. They decided that somehow the area where West was cleaning and painting had to be covered to allow work to be done on the bars and outside air vent. What if West sweeps the dirt down from the top of B-Block so it would land on the areas below, including cells as far down as Broadway? As the saying goes "the plot thickens." West did just that: the dirt came down and fell in some of the cells and on the floors below. There were three levels of cells from the top of B-Block to the main floor. The inmate cleaning the main part of Broadway started complaining about the dirt coming down. I think he probably was asked or told to complain but probably did not even know why. When West suggested to the Lieutenant that blankets could be hung to stop the dirt and dust from falling, and to prevent any paint from falling on the floor when the painting started later, the Lieutenant, then Acting Captain, approved hanging the blankets. Approximately 30 blankets were used to cover an area that was as big as a house. The blankets created a concern because the East Gun Gallery guard couldn't see in and the West Gun Gallery Guard was too far away. I thought to myself here is West with no supervision, on top of the cellhouse performing his duties, and he really couldn't be seen. I did not really think about a break or escape plan only that this was a poor security position to allow. The blankets also shaded any light that might normally reflect in. Another Lieutenant disagreed with the blankets and a power struggle evolved between the two Lieutenants. One saying they shouldn't be allowed up there and the other saying "I am the Acting Captain. I'll say what goes up there." The blankets remained. I strongly voiced my opinion, as did other guards, saying that they shouldn't be there and should be removed.

The other part of the breach of security and probably the major blunder was the fact that these blankets were allowed to remain up for months. I do not know the exact date they were first put up, but they remained there for many months, and were still hanging after the escape. I mentioned several times, as did other guards, that this was a breach of security. I did however, agree, as did other guards, that a few days would have been acceptable. To this day I do not fully understand why the blankets remained, and why anyone in a position of higher authority did not recognize the security implications. Maybe they did, and that would have even made matters worse. It really ticked me off that nobody would listen, and I got frustrated every time I saw them. I got to the point where I would go in and say "These God damn blankets are still up there" but that really didn't help. I was angry and upset with myself that I never put anything in writing, and accept that as a major mistake on my part. Everyone knew the blankets were there, including the Warden.

One evening, during the period the blankets were up, an inmate, Calloway, signaled that he wanted to see me. His cell was on the inside of C-Block near the cut off. I was leaving for the evening so I walked over to talk to him. He told me "Mr. Albright, there is something going on over there. I don't know what it is; but something is going on." I was surprised: Why would an inmate tell me this? I didn't want to look a gift horse in the mouth and I had no idea what he was talking about. I reported this and nothing was done. Again I didn't put it in writing and I have to accept responsibility for that. To not follow up on this was another blunder and breach of security.

Not inspecting and investigating a broken water pipe in the cellhouse, B-Block, that Officer Hermann and I found some time prior to the escape was another breach of security. Although I don't know, the pipe could easily have been broken by the inmate/s crawling up to the blanketed area to work on the escape route. It did occur after the last official standing count was taken.

A practice that was stopped after I arrived was the daily shakedown, by section, and checks of the numerous bars in the prison. Monetary cutbacks and not enough manpower is why this was not done.

The Bureau of Prisons downgraded Tower No. 2 from being manned 24/7 to only a day shift. The escape occurred during the hours when the tower wasn't manned. Tower No. 3, which was located back by the water tower, also wasn't manned and this is the route the inmates took to enter the bay.

During the time 5:30 P.M. to 7:00 P.M. each evening, inmates could play musical instruments in their cells. This probably helped cover any noise made as the three of them slowly and meticulously dug the opening in the back of their cells to get to the utility corridor and also after they were able to get the hole big enough to get to the corridor and up to the blanketed area to work on the escape route. The last standing head count was taken about 5:15 P.M. allowing them to start working on the opening and later to get to the blanketed area. The three inmates all had cells on the ground floor and they had to get to the third floor where the blankets and escape route were located. I do not believe all three of the inmates went up to the blanketed area together; but probably only one or two at a time.

It was obvious that these individuals spent months chipping at the crumbling air vent and wall located in the rear wall of their cell. They made realistic false vent/wall guards to conceal their work. Morris had an accordion and he put the accordion case in front of the air vent to help conceal what was being done. Obviously it worked. When they finally got through the enlarged vent holes in their cells and had a plan to cover the area up during the day where it would not be detected, they were able to enter the utility corridor and climb up the utility pipes to the top of the cell block during night hours and work on bending the bars beneath the air vent and loosening the bolts to the outside roof vent to prepare it for removal during the escape. The bolts held the vents which were set on top of the roof. I believe they easily stored other items to be used during the escape in 5-gallon buckets of paint. To handle the night counts in which the guard would walk by the cells and look in they also constructed life like dummy heads from soap, paper-mache, and concrete powder using real hair collected from the barber shop, probably by Clarence Anglin who worked there. I was amazed how life like they looked and was impressed with the manner in which they were constructed. In the evenings they went to the top of the cellhouse to work on the roof vents and whatever else they needed to get done for the escape. Before leaving the back of their cell, they carefully placed the life like heads in the bed in such a manner that the guards would not miss them during the night counts. Here occurred another breach of security. When the guard checked the cells to count the inmates, after lights were out, he was required not only to see the inmate but to see "skin and breathing;" a fact that obviously did not occur. The heads were so real looking it either fooled the guard or poor checks were made. Rounds were required several times each night and included head counts of the inmates while they were sleeping.

They completed their escape plan and during the early morning hours of June 11, 1962, Morris and the Anglin Brothers (John and Clarence) left their cells never to be seen again. They exited through the enlarged vent holes located in the rear wall of their cells, into the utility corridor, climbed the utility pipes to the blanketed area (and for the last time I will say those damn blankets) on top of the cellhouse, up through the bent bars below the vent, removed the outside vent, up through the opening, and across the roof, climbed down a drain pipe, across by the power house (northeast side of the island) and into the water using the crude life raft and crude vests they constructed. The life raft was made from raincoats and most likely was constructed and stored either in the blanket area or somewhere in the corridor. It was never really determined how many raincoats they got or why the accountability of these raincoats didn't ring a bell; however, every inmate had a raincoat issued to him and they were kept in their cell. Another blunder - accountability for the raincoats.

I was told later by an inmate that at about the same time as they would have been going across the roof, Lieutenant Wier was walking down Broadway to check the hospital and dining room. A loud noise was heard. That is when the outer air vent cover was probably taken off and it apparently made a loud noise when it fell to the roof. The noise certainly frightened the sea gulls causing them to fly off making a lot of noise. The tower reported the seagulls taking off; however, it was never investigated.

I guess if there was any justice at all in this escape it belonged to Allen West, the fourth inmate who was suppose to go out with the other three. He really fouled up and was unable to break out of his cell. He could not get out through the hole in the wall under his sink that he made to escape. It wasn't large enough. Had he not dug it out far enough to squeeze out? I have my own opinion: The other three cemented him in from the back, interesting thought. Another interesting thought, if the hole was not large enough for him to get out did he ever climb up to the blanketed area to help secure the escape route? What a shame, all his planning only to be left behind. West was put in segregation, the Dark Hole, and remained there until the prison closed. He was transferred to the Federal Prison at McNeil, Washington. I heard he later died in a Florida Prison.

I learned that when they took the morning count at about 7:00 A.M. the guard came back and told the Lieutenant he had a couple inmates who didn't stand for the count. The Lieutenant said "We will see about that!" He went back with the guard to Anglin's cell and said "Get up." There was no movement. The Lieutenant reached down and hit the head and it went off the bunk onto the floor. It was now a reality that an escape had occurred or possibly might be in progress. They also noticed that the other Anglin brother was also missing. The brothers were in cells side by side. They realized that another inmate was gone when inmate West said: "You should check the one next to me. They went off and left me." That was Morris' cell and West knew he was also gone.

The alarm was sounded shortly after they discovered the missing inmates. Once they found out what occurred they immediately searched the area including the cells. The search revealed the tools they used, fake heads, wall openings, bent air vents, and the outside air vent that was removed. An inspection of all the cells was also started and in one cell they found some hack saw blades embedded in the walls. The inmates assigned to the cell didn't even know they were there. Searches of everything throughout the prison continued for sometime, and as late as September several bread slice blades were found concealed in a corner of one of the cells, fastened to the wall with tape covered over with soap, then painted to blend in with the wall making it unnoticeable until the cell paint was scraped off. It was John Anglin's cell and I thought to myself; "They inspected his cell before, how did they miss it?" In February 1963, while dismantling vacant cells, two separate pieces of shelving had been found with concealed contraband. The wood shelving had been "holed" out with contraband placed inside the hole, then filled up with soap, and a very careful paint job made it literally impossible to detect anything wrong through normal visual inspection. I wasn't surprised as the more I learned the more I could see just how creative the inmates were. Amazing!

I know the Warden, Associate Warden, Captain, and Lieutenants were talking and asking questions, investigating. There were several counts taken during the evening and obviously the dummy heads were counted and the number of inmates counted was correct each time. It was also obvious that the counts were flawed and the guard's responsibility to see "skin and breathing" didn't occur. I knew one guard who would disgust other guards when he relieved them. It would take him forever to do the count.

He would watch for "skin and breathing" where others just routinely went by and counted heads. Sometimes they had to hold the boat to take the shift back to Fort Mason because he was still counting. I hate to admit it but I personally did it both ways.

On the night of the escape I was placed on roof detail after night fell, with a pistol and flashlight. I couldn't flash very often because of limited mobility with crutches. Finally, the Lieutenant sent a relief to take my place and I was assigned to the control center. I probably would have been better off on the roof because it was so busy in the control center with constant phone calls from all over. I forwarded them to the Warden's secretary who would occasionally forward them to the Captain.

The guard who counted the inmates on the night and morning rounds took the rap. In the upper echelons, I don't believe anyone did. There were clues or warnings and many mistakes and blunders, many that I was aware of. In a way I am ashamed that I didn't pursue them stronger or put them in writing, especially the blankets and being told of something going on by one of the inmates. I was disappointed that it occurred during the time I was there.

The inmates had a field day teasing, laughing, comments, etc., toward the guards in the immediate time after the escape. Although it tapered off as time went on, I wasn't too happy about their attitude, whether we deserved it or not.

I believe two life vests and letters/photographs belonging to the Anglin Brothers were found in the waters in the bay and outside the Golden Gate Bridge in a water proof container; however, no sign or trace of the men were ever found. A man's body, dressed in clothing similar to the prison uniform was found on the coast near San Francisco. The body was so badly deteriorated it could not be identified. I wonder, with today's technology why don't they dig up the body that was found and do DNA tests.

The water in the Bay is cold and the temperature averages 50-55 degrees Fahrenheit. Additionally, the distance to shore is at least 1 and one quarter miles with extremely strong currents.

Depending on ones definition of escape, Morris and the Anglin Brothers were successful; but their survival is highly questionable and I will not accept the fact that they are somewhere out there, alive, until one or all three of them come forward. No trace was ever found of any of them and I completely agree that they drowned in the strong current and cold waters that surrounded Alcatraz. It was reported shortly after the escape, that a ship saw a body floating with clothing like the prisoner's wore; however, they didn't pick it up and it couldn't be located later. I also think that if they were alive today, or escaped, their egos would be so large that they would tell someone, report it to the press, or give themselves up for the publicity. Imagine them coming forward and saying "We made it. We were the first and only inmates to escape from Alcatraz." Would they be prosecuted? I don't think so. However big dollars would be available – movies, articles, books, talk shows, etc. If they did escape, how could they keep quiet. Will we ever really know?

My suspicions are that there were three escapees with one small poorly constructed raft. I strongly feel the Anglin brothers probably killed Morris to lessen the weight on the raft, and they in turn drowned and got washed out to sea. I also believe if Allen West had gone out too, he would have ended up dead at the hand of the Anglin Brothers. Extensive tests of the escape route were conducted, using the same conditions, and it was concluded they didn't make it.

To conclude, there were many factors that I briefly outlined that I feel led to and played significant roles in this escape; including insufficient security, budget cuts, a deteriorating prison, major blunders by prison officials, breaches of security, and a lack of follow-up on information. Coupling these, with the ingenious planning and execution on the part of the four inmates, it was not only possible for an escape to occur but was a definite contribution. I think about it even after all these years and realize that I too was a part of all this. I feel that these inmates set the traps that we all fell for, and then took advantage of the opportunities and security breaches we presented.

Although the movie starring Clint Eastwood called "Escape from Alcatraz" made the escape even more famous, it also pointed out the deteriorating conditions of the prison. The movie showed them escaping off Broadway and that is not correct. In real life they escaped through the roof of B block. It probably looked better to have them on Broadway in the movie. Additionally, in the movie there was a scene that showed Eastwood looking very seriously as if he wanted to steal a pair of fingernail clippers that was setting on the Warden's desk. This would not have been necessary as each inmate was issued a pair of fingernail clippers when they first arrive at the Prison.

After the escape, paranoia set in. One evening when reporting for duty in the control room I noticed some "white dust droplets" on top of the desk. I looked up at the ceiling and noticed that the droplets matched the ceiling tile. My immediate thought was that someone might be trying to get into the control center through the ceiling. I had the main gate officer come in to cover for me and I handed him my pistol. I climbed up, removed several tiles, and with my flashlight looked around the ceiling area. I saw nothing out of order or suspicious. This was during the 4 P.M. to midnight shift and it was quite dark. I assumed it was caused by a sonic boom from an aircraft. I logged it in the control center log.

I will say without any doubt in my mind, that it was this escape that shattered the reputation of Alcatraz as being escape proof.

CHAPTER TWENTY-TWO

On December 16, 1962, at 5:47 P.M. I was working in the control center. Lieutenant Robbins called on the emergency phone (RED PHONE) from the kitchen. I often wondered what I would do if that phone ever rang. I did realize that I had to immediately log the time of the call. Robbins said "Jim, I got a couple missing from the kitchen basement, get me some help." He told me they were inmates Parker (AZ 1413) and Scott (AZ 1403), two kitchen orderlies. Cullen, the Main Gate Guard, was at the control center about to make a cellhouse check. I said to him "You run and get the Warden, we're missing a couple of inmates." I then notified the island launch which was near Fort Mason and it began checking the water along the beaches around the island. Cullen ran across the street to the warden's home and informed him. Warden Blackwell came immediately and asked what happened. I explained what Lieutenant Robbins told me. I asked him if he would like me to sound the alarm and he said "No, let me do it." The prison plan to deal with an escape was put into effect at 5:57 P.M. Two special counts of all the inmates were taken; one at 6:00 P.M. and another at 7:35 P.M. Both confirmed that only Parker and Scott were missing. The Warden turned the speakers on to all departments and residents directing island employees to report up top. In the meantime I was calling the Associate Warden and Captain. I dialed the phone number listed for the Captain and the voice on the phone said "Mahoney." It was Pat Mahoney the boat operator. I said "Oh shit Pat. I am trying to get the Captain." Pat informed me that the captain recently moved and he helped me get the correct number. I informed him that he better get up here anyway because we would need the boat moved as two inmates were missing. I called the Associate Warden and Captain and informed them of what had occurred.

About this time island employees started coming in and activity picked-up. I issued weapons and keys to guards who were assigned to man the towers, let authorized employees in and out of the main gate, handled the boat radio, alerted the tower guards, and other things. It was very hectic but because of prior training and experience it went rather smoothly. The island employees were well trained and knew where they were to go and what they were to do. The Captain assigned armed guards around the island and said to me "Jim you write down what time everybody comes in and what time they leave." I told him "Yes, sir." Anyway, I was as busy as a beaver, working fast and hard. Finally, Lieutenant Mills was assigned to help me.

Armed guards were immediately assigned to Towers 2, 3 and 4 and I issued weapons and ammunition before they went to man the towers. The towers were not manned as they were never manned at night. This is another of the many cutbacks that adversely affected the effective running of the prison. The two guards sent to towers 3 and 4 were the Picken brothers, Darrell to 3 tower and Don to 4 tower. They were talking back and forth on the intercom and their conversations could be heard in the control center. They were yelling and shouting "Look here, look there!" Other guards were cutting in with, "What do you see?" I had to be aggressive and tell them "Hey, you guys have to shut-up, I can't hear." I later apologized to the

Tower officers for yelling at them. Shortly thereafter, Officer Darrell Pickens reported that a man was sighted on "Little Alcatraz" - a small rock outcropping right off the old industries building. This was at approximately 6:02 P.M. The Alcatraz launch was sent around to check the report. Both Darrell and Don had fired ONE warning shot each. I have read books and heard stories that many shots were fired; however, they are not correct as I issued the ammunition and know that all ammunition was returned except for one shell from each of the Picken brothers.

The boat found Parker on Little Alcatraz, alive, and he was picked up at 6:10 P.M. When they picked him up they tied his hands and legs so he couldn't move. Parker had gotten scared after jumping into the water and held up on Little Alcatraz. He stated he couldn't swim. He was put on the boat by the guards and returned to the dock. I was told later that they hog tied him and carried him by the rope.

The outside world quickly responded and the phones starting ringing, from all over. The emergency alarm was not sounded as we were getting all the help needed by just having the island employees report up top.

In the meantime we had Parker, got him to the island hospital, checked him over and took him down and locked him in the "Dark Hole." The boats were still patrolling and I thought: Where is Scott? I had already notified the Coast Guard, San Francisco Police, Presidio Police, and sheriff so that they could be alerted and watching.

The Presidio desk Sergeant reported that a man had been located and picked-up on the rock at Fort Point, a little old fort underneath the Golden Gate Bridge, at approximately 7:15 P.M. Shortly therafter, at 8:10 P.M., it was reported that it was Scott and that he was in their custody. They further reported that he was found by several teenagers who were down at Fort Point. They reported seeing a male body wash up and it was "naked as a jaybird." They called the Presidio Police who went and investigated. Scott was barely alive and nearly frozen to death. I thought "Wow, if he hadn't been almost frozen to death he probably would have overpowered the teenagers and took their car and be gone." A floatation device made out of rubber gloves and other material was also found. It was made from rubber gloves that Scott probably stole from the hospital where he worked. It further shows just how creative these inmates could be. The Coast Guard stepped in, treated Scott, and took him to Letterman Army Hospital in Presidio where he was treated for shock and hypothermia. Scott survived and was returned to Alcatraz, at about 9:55 P.M. where he was taken to the administrative office. He was back in the main cellhouse at 10:48 P.M. I was extremely pleased that only five hours and one minute had elapsed since the escape was reported to me and both inmates were back in the confines of Alcatraz. The emergency was called off at 9:02 P.M. by order of Captain Welch.

Lieutenant Delmore informed me that the two inmates went out through the last window at the East end of the kitchen basement. They cut the bars and detention sash that surrounded the window, climbed out, went up and over the roof, and down to the water by Tower #2 which was unmanned during hours of darkness. They used scouring powder on a string to cut the bars on the window, to enable them to be bent. I know this works as I had cut pipe that way myself. The discovery took place when Howard Waldron, Food Services Supervisor, who was once a guard but switched to food service, went down to the kitchen basement to get something to bring up to prepare for meals. When he came back up he asked Lieutenant Robbins "Aren't we suppose to have a couple of men down stairs? There is nobody down there." Robbins went down and sure enough nobody was there. The two inmates, Parker and Scott, were assigned to food services to do various jobs. If Howard hadn't noticed them missing, it could have been another 15 minutes or so before the escape attempt was discovered. They had to have been spending time cutting the window bars for some time. The bars should have been checked periodically and any cutting would have been detected. Because of cuts in the prison budget, this is another example of the reduced security.

I recorded only ½ hour of overtime on the evening watch because by 12:30 in the morning not much was going on. Things were back to normal, or as normal as they got on Alcatraz. Until the end of my shift I received and routed calls to the Warden's secretary, from all over the world – London, Paris, Argentina!

As Control Center Officer, I sent the following memorandum dated December 16, 1962, to Warden Blackwell through Captain Welch in reference to the attempted escape of 1413 Parker and 1403 Scott:

"The 5:28 P.M. count was OK and the 5:40 P.M. launch left on schedule.

At 5:47 P.M. December 16, 1962 Lt. Robbins called the Control Center on the Emergency #222 phone stating two inmates 1403 Scott and 1413 Parker were missing, and he would need some help.

I sent Mr. Cullen the Main Gate Officer, who was about to leave the Administrative building to make a trip around the cellhouse for a security check, to get Warden Blackwell. I then notified the island launch which was near Ft. Mason, and it returned to start checking the water along the beaches around the island.

The escape plans were put into effect at approx. 5:57 P.M. Military and Civilian authorities notified at 6:20 P.M.

Armed officers were put in #2, 3, & 4 towers. Officer Darrell Pickens who was in #3 tower reported a man sighted on Little Alcatraz at approximately 6:02 P.M. The Alcatraz launch was sent around to check the report out. #3 tower Darrell Pickens and #4 tower Don Pickens fired one warning shot each. The boat found 1413 Parker on Little Alcatraz and he was picked up 6:10 P.M. It was reported to me by Lt. Delmore that the two inmates went out through the last window at the East end of the Kitchen basement, by cutting the bars and detention sash. Two special counts were taken, 12 – 16 – 62. One at 6:00 P.M. and one at 7:35 P.M. The Presido desk Sergeant reported they had a man on the rock at Ft. Point San Francisco at approx. 7:15 P.M.; the call was switched immediately to the Warden. At 8:10 P.M. it was reported to me that 1403 Scott had been picked up at Ft. Point, San Francisco. The emergency was called off effective at 9:02 P.M. by order of Captain Welch. 1403 Scott in

*administrative office at 9:55 P.M. and into Main Cellhouse at
10:48 P.M. All weapons turned in and accounted for."*

A daily log book was maintained in the control center. When I reported to work that day (shift was 4:00 P.M. to Midnight) I "pre-marked" in the log book. "12/16/62" - dropped down a couple lines and put "Routine Watch" - dropped down a couple more lines and signed my name. I would occasionally do this so I wouldn't leave and forget to log out. I realized that I had done this when I was heading off watch. I told my relief, "Wait a minute I forgot that damn log." I looked at the log and it said "Routine Watch." I said to my self "escape on a routine watch? That won't do!" Then I put "until 5:47 pm when all hell broke loose." The next day I went to work and the Captain called and said "Mr. Albright did you sign the log last night." I said, "Yes, sir." He then said, "You didn't sign it earlier did you." I replied "No sir, you are to sign that at the end of the shift." I knew that the Captain knew I was not telling the truth. Needless to say I never did that again, as that was a lesson well learned.

This was the second of the two escapes that occurred while I was on Alcatraz and probably cemented the decision to close the "ROCK." This was an attempt, not an escape, as both inmates were caught. Had Scott not been washed up on the rocks at Fort Point he would probably have been washed out to sea. He is the only inmate known to make it to shore alive. This made me wonder "Could the Anglin brothers or Morris have made it?" Although everything indicates it is highly unlikely, it raises a doubt.

This escape was the last major event I encountered. When I thought about what I had experienced so far, it made me reflect on family life on Alcatraz. It was great!

CHAPTER TWENTY-THREE

Little did we realize that living on Alcatraz would be one of the most memorable and enjoyable times of our lives. But this wasn't something we knew at first, and although Cathy, Kenny and I were excited about moving to the island, we had no idea what to expect and a lot of questions needed to be answered. What would life be like living in a closed community with everybody working or living there, except the inmates, and had one primary purpose, supporting the operation of a maximum security prison? I knew the rules and regulations for the guards and inmates, but what would the rules and regulations be for my family? Cathy had all the right questions, but I had very few answers. We joked about sharing an address with America's most hardened and notorious criminals. Thoughts ran through our minds about school, medical care, mail, social life, things to do for the children, the living quarters, and life in general. We had talked to other families who lived on the island, and although they answered some of our questions, we both realized that there were many still unanswered. Also, there would be nuances that we would have to adjust to. We were extremely pleased by the positive comments from other inhabitants about life on Alcatraz and that made us feel a lot better. It took very little time to find out what living on Alcatraz was all about, and most of our questions were quickly and easily answered. Life on Alcatraz was not only the right decision but it was exciting and rewarding.

Anyone who worked on the island had the opportunity to live on Alcatraz when quarters became available. I was really surprised at the total number of apartment buildings and other housing that was available, and to learn that about one third of the employees and their families resided on Alcatraz. The south end of the island was where most of the housing was located. Clustered about an old army parade ground were three of the four apartment buildings - buildings A, B, and C - with the fourth, Building 64, located above the Dock. In addition to the apartments, there were four cottages – one for the Business Manager, two for the Lieutenants, and one for the Food Services Supervisor as well as a duplex for the Associate Warden and the Captain. Two separate, but beautiful homes were "up on top." These were for the Warden and the Medical Technician Associate. Finally, two apartments were located in the light house where two Coast Guard families resided. Building A contained the bachelor quarters; however, several married couples with no children also lived there. All housing except A Building, the light house, and the buildings located "on top" were fenced in for security reasons and could be locked in case of an escape or emergency. Keys to the apartments and fenced in area were issued to all the residents and we could freely move about whenever we wanted.

Our first apartment was a one bedroom (#108) in Building 64. After the birth of our first daughter, Vicki, we moved to a two bedroom apartment (#302) in the same building. Shortly before the island closed, we moved to Building C – Apartment C202 - a two bedroom apartment with a fireplace and a great view of San Francisco and the Golden Gate Bridge. Cathy said "What a beautiful and different view looking toward San Francisco instead of looking from San Francisco."

Living on Alcatraz was about the same as living in a small town. Even though big city conveniences were not far away, it required following a boat schedule and going on a short boat trip. There were also significant differences. To start with, and probably the most significant was a set of "Regulations for Island Residents" issued by Warden Madigan. They weren't that difficult to follow but they were strictly enforced. Cathy and I spent many hours making sure we fully understood them.

Located on the ground floor of Building 64, in addition to the Post Office, was a small grocery that carried items such as meat, milk, bread, canned products, etc. All other goods had to be purchased from the mainland. A church was located on top of Building C and a pistol range for the officers was located above the old tunnel near the dock. A speaker system was located throughout the island and it was loud enough for residents to hear. Prison officials could make announcements, if necessary.

Trash and garbage was picked up by civilian workers. I was told that historically two inmates, accompanied by an officer, at first performed this function but it was before we arrived. Harold Miller, a guard, and close friend of ours told me that when he was escorting two inmates on trash detail, they grabbed him, tied him up, threw him in some weeds on the East Beach and attempted to escape. Shortly thereafter, the use of inmates to collect the trash was discontinued and replaced with civilian workers. Also, items considered contraband, such as knives, etc., could not be put in the trash and used razor blades were dropped in a slot in the back of the medicine cabinet in the apartment, for obvious reasons.

Minor medical concerns were handled by the prison doctor; otherwise we had health insurance coverage with Kaiser. A one time $1.00 registration fee was paid the first time we visited a doctor and thereafter, a monthly fee took care of all other medical issues and costs. The delivery of a baby, for example, cost $60.00 and that was for everything including after care, return visits, etc. It did require a trip to San Francisco to visit the facility. Cathy stated that the only time she was a little worried was when she was pregnant with Vicki. However, I had obtained permission before hand for a special boat, if needed, to take her to the mainland. All we had to do was call the boat officer. Our two daughters, Vicki and Donna, were born while we lived on the island and the medical care was outstanding.

Things that happen in any household such as a broken pipe, plumbing issues, electrical issues, etc., were handled by the island mechanical services. Plumbers, electricians, carpenters, and laborers were always available and the service provided on the island was outstanding. Some of these professionals lived on the island.

This was a close community; however, sometimes we would laugh about just how close it occasionally seemed. Someone on the island always knew what you were doing and where you were going. Cathy would occasionally make cookies and would put them on the kitchen window sill to cool. On one occasion she received a call from an individual who did not identify himself saying: "I see you made cookies, I will be right over." Surprised by the call, she was a little shaken until she discovered it was Herman Boonie, the guard in the Officer's mess. He could see our kitchen window and saw the cookies. He also told me: "Oh your wife is baking cookies." I didn't think much about it and when I finished work and went to my apartment, there was Officer Boonie drinking coffee, eating cookies, and chatting with Cathy.

Officer Boonie was an interesting and friendly guard who everyone liked. He would go across the playground with a box of candy and the kids would follow him, like the piped piper. Another person who would tell me when Cathy made cookies was the inmate who worked in the officer's mess. He also could look down and see the kitchen window in our apartment and he would tell me she made cookies. Another incident I remember was when an inmate cook in the office's mess told me: "Your boy crawled on that railing, you had better watch him. He could get hurt." I thanked him and thought "You know he probably has a family and cares." Inmates working on the dock saw everybody who came and left and occasionally would tell me that "your wife went to town." Cathy stated: "I don't worry, they're up there and I am down here. If they want to get out they're not going to want to stay on the island, but get off."

There was one occasion involving a possible escape attempt. Cathy had taken Kenny and Vicki to visit Betty Miller in her apartment and while there the whistle went off indicating an escape. That also meant that wherever you were you had to stay and Cathy and the children remained at Betty's apartment. Shortly thereafter an officer came around, identified himself, came in and actually went through Miller's apartment in detail, making sure they were not being held hostage. He then checked all the apartments including ours, and when he was satisfied there was nobody there, he escorted Cathy, Vicki, and Kenny back to our apartment.

One draw back that the island had which both Cathy and I hated were the mice, cockroaches, bugs and ants that seemed to be plentiful and multiply. It was definitely a breeding ground. One of the worst I'd ever seen. We sprayed frequently and you could always tell when someone sprayed because the cockroaches would take refuge in other apartments. If you didn't spray often they would return quickly. My family had an incident when we went on vacation. Before we left, Kenny took a sucker from one of the kitchen drawers, licked it, and put it back in the drawer. Neither Cathy or I was aware of this, and when we returned from vacation and went to the kitchen there was a trail of ants coming from outside across the kitchen floor, up the cabinet, into the drawer, and another trail of ants was coming right back out of the drawer. When Cathy opened the cabinet they were feasting on the sucker. Spraying throughout the prison facilities was frequent and thorough, but this didn't stop them. I remember one time when they didn't spray the store room. It cost material and money as a lot of items had to be replaced. I thought "These bugs must really like living on Alcatraz."

Cathy stated that living here didn't make her feel as confined as when in San Francisco. She didn't drive and that made things more difficult when we lived on the mainland. Also, in San Francisco she didn't allow Kenny to be outside by himself. With no yard to play in and the closest play area several blocks away, Cathy either had to go with him or he stayed home. Here there was a safe playing area and most importantly he could go out and play without Cathy having to walk a long distance. Frequently when Cathy took Kenny to the playground other women were there with their children, and Cathy could sit and talk.

The playground area was an old parade ground, made of concrete, and located close to the housing areas. It contained a handball court, two sandboxes – one on both sides of the handball court, a swing set, slide, teeter-totter, and basketball hoop. It was a big empty space and the children would play softball, kickball, basketball, and handball. Some of the children had roller skates and would skate around the grounds. Others would take shirts and sheets and use them for sails and let the wind whip them across the playground. Children could also play at night. Lights were located on the handball court and surrounded the cottages. Kenny liked playing with his truck in the sandbox. He had to wear special arch support shoes and would go out, take them off in the sandbox, and use them for a shovel. He would occasionally leave them there when he came in and we would have to go back and get them. However, everything wasn't perfect. There was a yard wall very close to the parade ground and it was about a foot wide and 3 ½ feet tall. In some places it would drop straight down to rocks. Children will be children and although told not to, occasionally someone would get up and walk on the wall. Once in a while Cathy or I would see someone and go and tell them to get down. I do not believe anyone ever fell off but the risk was there and Kenny knew without a doubt what our feelings were. A walkway to the East Beach was also close and kids were not allowed to go down to the beach area. That is where I found a body one night. It was a person who had jumped off the Golden Gate Bridge and had washed up on the beach.

Kenny had a lot of friends and they played together both inside and out. Once, Kenny and one of his friends, Shawn Rodgers, found some paint and decided to paint the Lieutenant's house. This occurred shortly before the island closed. Although a serious prank, it wasn't serious enough to have them committed as inmates to Alcatraz. Another incident involved a young boy who lived next door to us. He was a boy scout and his assignment for the scouts was to cook something. He put the food item he was preparing in the oven to cook and it caught on fire. He came running over to our back door and told me he had a fire. I ran over and the first thing I saw was some smoke and cockroaches running about. Apartments had fire extinguishers and I grabbed theirs and put the fire out. The cause of the fire was mice. They had built a nest in the oven and it caught on fire.

One of the most rewarding aspects of living on the island was how friendly and helpful everyone was. They looked out for each other. Steve Mahoney and Kenny were close friends, and Cathy took care of Steve because Anna Mahoney worked in San Francisco and Pat Mahoney was the boat officer. Both were little boys who got into a lot of things including trouble, but nothing serious. When someone needed something there was always a person available. They would say "Don't worry about it. I'll take care of it."

Much of the social life centered around getting together with families and friends or at the Officers Club, which was also used as a social hall. The club contained a small soda bar, library, large dining/dance room, ping pong table and a bowling alley. The large dining/dance floor was used for retirement or transfer dinners, bingo and holiday dances. Movies were shown there every Sunday night, after the inmates had seen them on Saturday and Sunday afternoon. I learned how to run the movie projector and showed the movies. They would be sent back to the mainland on the midnight boat. A two lane bowling alley was located inside the officers club and it could be used any time. Special events were sponsored throughout the year. These events included an annual picnic, an annual ice cream and watermelon feast, held on the parade grounds; a Frontier Days celebration and Christmas party. Most of the time food and drinks were provided free by the Officers Club and families would also bring pot luck, cookies, etc. Ruppert Sutton, the food services supervisor for the prison loved to help out on all functions and that was really appreciated by everyone. To raise money for these functions the officer's club sponsored fund raising events. Normally we brought our own bottle and the club would have the set ups available. A fee of $2.00 was paid to help offset those costs.

Shortly after the island closed, the Officer's Club was disbanded and the money left in the treasury was used to purchase a watch for each officer with their name and dates inscribed thereon. I received my watch just prior to leaving the island and it is still in my possession.

Children were not allowed to play with toy guns or have them on the island for obvious reasons; however, one exception was made each year when the residence would celebrate Frontier Days. It was like cowboy days. The island residents provided the entertainment. One of the guards lived up the coast and would bring a Boy Scout Group to the island. They dressed in real Indian clothing. They did traditional Indian dances and had a good time. We enjoyed their company. Children could have toy wooden guns at this function and that was the only time they were allowed on the island. They had to be taken from the island after the function. One of the most exciting events at the Frontier Day celebration were the plays that the children put on. The families really looked forward to these shows.

On Christmas Eve anyone who wanted Santa Claus to deliver presents to their children would leave the presents outside their front door and L.B. Davis, Superintendent of Industries would dress up as Santa, pick-up the presents, put them in his bag and deliver them to the kids. Cathy and I made an old 8mm movie of Santa delivering Kenny's present and the joy of seeing Kenny run to him, eyes big and smiling. We still have that movie. Additionally, each year a Christmas pageant was put on by the children in the social hall.

There was a Ladies Club that met several times a month. Cathy said they would sit around and discuss things to do, places to go, and basically anything of interest. Sometimes they would have a lunch or just get together for coffee.

All comings and goings from and to the island were dictated by the boat schedule. Passengers were not allowed to enter the dock area until 10 minutes before the boat departed, and would sit in the dock office until the boat whistle sounded (normally 5 minutes before departure). From the housing area they would go down to the gate by Tower #1, the tower officer would recognize who was there and unlock the gate (electronically) so they could proceed to the dock. However, he would not do this earlier than 10 minutes prior to the boat's departure and hollering "5 on the line." Neither the boat schedule nor the regulations created problems for us, just a little inconvenience at times.

The "Warden Johnston" ferried kids to San Francisco for school. Kenny went to Sherman public school in San Francisco and I would take him over before my shift started. When Warden Blackwell became warden he added a two o'clock early morning boat trip so island residents could remain in town longer. If it was real foggy the island residents would be somewhat concerned as the boat, at first didn't have radar. As the boat would get closer to the island the boat captain would sound his horn and the sound would bounce off the rocks. This would enable him to tell how close he was getting. Sometimes the people on the island would bang on pots and pans on the dock so he could hear them and find his way in. They ended up getting radar later and that was well received by everyone including the residents.

The dock at Fort Mason was a floating dock and one time one of the guards, Lee Schima, and his son were returning from town with a new colored TV. He was carrying it down the stairs of the dock when a swell came up and the dock went up and down and out a little and the stairs went down between the dock and they went right into the water TV and all. Some of the people who were there helped fish them and the TV out of the water. They picked the TV up and took it to get fixed.

When Cathy was returning to the island with our new daughter, Vicki Lynn (only 48 hours after she was born), we were at the dock in Fort Mason, getting ready to return to the island and the water was extremely rough. When Cathy started down the steps, the floating dock went out and she couldn't see the steps. The boat officer came and took Vicki Lynn out of her arms and put her on the boat. The Boat Officer and I lifted Cathy onto the boat.

I enjoyed the time I had with my family on Alcatraz. We took advantage of the big city environment by occasionally visiting San Francisco for fun and pleasure, in addition to shopping. Some trips were for sightseeing, such as visiting the Golden Gate Park and the grassy marina; while other trips included dinners and shows. The kids enjoyed playing games on the mainland, especially as there was grass.

An island's newspaper "The Fog Horn" was published monthly and was an informal channel of communication. It included rumors and gossip. It was only for the staff and was not given to the prisoners. Inmates did not see it except for a couple who helped put it together. The warden's secretary was responsible for publishing, although a lot of people provided input. Every staff member and employee was encouraged to submit articles about themselves. I never did. Guards would on occasions take it to work to read and an inmate might read over his shoulder but would not take it.

About 3 or 4 times a year, fishing on Alcatraz was a major attraction and event for island residents. This excluded inmates, of course. During these times fish were highly visible in the waters surrounding Alcatraz, and they were plentiful. A list of people who wanted to be notified when the fish were running was posted in the dock office. Some only wanted to be called during certain hours and some anytime. A lot depended on what shift a person worked. The list would include guards, officers, service workers, and any island residents. Once notification went out that the fish were running, within a relatively short period of time 30 or more people would be fishing. They might fish off the East Beach, the Industries, or on the Dock. There was no limit on how many you could catch. Due to the large number of fish that were caught, a chute was built that went from the dock into the water, with a water hose hooked to it. The caught fish were then laid on the chute, cleaned and filleted. The carcasses would go down the chute and into the water. The sea gulls would have a picnic and before the carcasses hit the water they would nab them. Fish filets would be lying all over the place and anyone could help themselves to all they wanted. Good eating! The fish were white fish. On the West coast of the United States they are called striped bass, and I understand that on the East Coast they are called Rock fish; however, they are the same. The fish remaining after everyone got what they wanted would be taken to the cellhouse and put in a freezer for the inmates. The inmates loved them. This also helped the kitchen food steward by saving money and he could then put on better meals, such as steak instead of hamburger.

When I started my guard duties at Alcatraz, my family included Cathy and Kenny. When I left the island in June 1963, it also included Vicki and Donna. Their birth certificates indicate "Alcatraz" as their place of birth. Wouldn't it be a great trivia question: "Who was the last child born on Alcatraz when it was an operating prison?

Of course I know the answer – "Donna Albright."

CHAPTER TWENTY-FOUR

I thought long and hard of what to say about the closing of Alcatraz because even thinking about it brings back so many memories and a lump in my throat. It seems like yesterday. There I was living in a small town in Aurora, Colorado, opening a letter from the U.S. Government which stated "congratulations" you have been selected for a position in the Federal Prison system at "U.S.P. Alcatraz." The next thing I know Cathy, Kenny and I are there with a lot of anticipation and apprehension. Now the journey has ended and it was time to go. I remember thinking to myself, "What a trip and experience I just had," working on Alcatraz, living on the island, and two great additions to our family; Vicki and Donna."

Well, the closing of Alcatraz started to unfold as the facility slowly deteriorated and the expense of operating this Maximum Security Prison became prohibitive. Maintenance, repairs, adequate staffing and housing the inmates were driving the costs of operations to an extremely high level. From my understanding, Alcatraz was approximately three times more expensive to operate than other

Federal Prisons. The obvious answer was to close Alcatraz! I think the closure was moved up on the priority list with the escape of Morris-Anglin Brothers on June 11, 1962, and the Parker-Scott attempted escape on December 16, 1962. The decision to close the Federal Prison at Alcatraz came as no surprise to anyone; however, it was a disappointment to many, including myself. Attorney General Robert Kennedy made the final decision.

Around August 1962, rumors were spreading like the cockroaches on the island that Alcatraz may be closing. These rumors came to reality in early September 1962. Officers from the Bureau of Prisons in Washington D.C. came to Alcatraz and interviewed the island staff regarding transfers. We were given an opportunity to list three prisons where our transfer could take us. I listed two, one in Arizona and one in Texas. When the transfer list came out in early 1963, I learned that I was being transferred to Marion, Illinois. I didn't particularly like the selection; however, I realized that one doesn't always get what one wants. Later, after reporting to the Federal prison in Marion, I learned the reason why I ended up there. I went to the Federal prison in Atlanta, Georgia for training and had the opportunity to meet with the warden, Warden Blackwell, who was transferred to Atlanta from Alcatraz. I had a most pleasant talk with him, and in addition to discussing Alcatraz, he told me that he initially thought he was going to Marion, Illinois, from Alcatraz. He stated he picked me, along with several other Alcatraz officers, to join him there. It made me feel very good that a person of his status would want me to be part of his team. Another good feeling came when he offered me the opportunity to join him at the Atlanta prison. I declined the offer as my family and I were now established in Marion and another move wasn't too inviting.

With the decision reached to close the Rock, the next step was to move the inmates to other Federal Prisons. This started on September 10, 1962 when the first group of 6 inmates were transferred to Leavenworth, Kansas. An additional 16 were scheduled to be airlifted at the same time; however, that was postponed until October, after the first group was successfully completed. At the end of October, 232 inmates remained. The movement of inmates continued and by the end of January 1963, only 118 remained; and on March 21, 1963, the day the Federal Penitentiary was officially closed, the last 27 inmates left Alcatraz. The last inmate meal served on Alcatraz was breakfast on March 21st. I've had people ask: "Who was the last inmate to leave?" Well, it was Weatherman (AZ 1576). I remember Weatherman's comments as he departed: "Alcatraz has never been no good for nobody."

The process of moving the inmates is a story in itself. The inmates were taken to other prisons by "inmate chains" which normally consisted of 32 prisoners chained together. I thought that the inmates would be jumping at the bit to get out of Alcatraz; however, most of them wanted to be in the last chain to leave. Each chain was escorted by six guards. Several guards were brought in from other prisons to assist in the movement. I was assigned to go with the first chain and along with the other escorting officers we reported to the cellhouse at approximately 4:00 A.M. of the day the chain was to leave. The inmates were escorted to the dining room for breakfast; then to the clothing room for a thorough strip search by the MTA, followed by being "dressed out" and chained with leg irons, belly chains and hand cuffs. After being loaded on the prison bus and taken to the dock, they boarded the "Warden Blackwell" for the short trip to Fort Mason. The boat "Warden Johnston" was earlier replaced and was no longer in use by the Alcatraz boat fleet. I often wondered what thoughts went through the inmates' minds as they boarded and could look back at Alcatraz as they traveled across the waters to Fort Mason. After arrival between piers 2 and 3 at the dock in Fort Mason, the convicts were placed on a commercial bus and driven to the San Francisco Auxiliary Airport where they boarded the plane for the trip.

On each chain going out one officer was assigned to search the bus for anything, i.e., paper clips, straight pins, etc., to ensure that there was nothing the inmates could get their hands on and possibly use to pick a lock or attempt an escape. While this was being done another officer was searching the boat for the same reason. At Fort Mason, before the inmates were allowed to board the bus for the trip to the airport, the commercial bus was also thoroughly searched.

At the airport the inmates were held on the bus until the plane was thoroughly searched. We all knew how creative the inmates could be, and when the boarding was taking place I remembered an earlier incident when I was experimenting with getting out of handcuffs. I was on watch in the control center and in one of the desk drawers there was contraband (shakedown items found on inmates). The contraband included a piece of razor blade (1/8 inch wide) with tape on one end as a handle which I was told could be used as a pick to open handcuffs. Well, it was about 1:00 A.M. and things were quiet. Given the fact that I had very little experience with handcuffs, I decided to take a set of handcuffs, put the keys on the desk along with the razor blade (pick), put the handcuffs on, lock them and see if I could get them open with the pick. I never had handcuffs on and I really didn't know what to expect. I took the razor (lock pick) and in less than 20 seconds had the handcuffs off. It seemed too easy and I thought "I didn't dead lock them." Dead lock means putting the cuffs on and locking them using a little pin on the handcuffs which when pushed in secures them. Anyway, I put the handcuffs back on and dead locked them. I then took my hands and banged the desk. This loosened the dead lock and again I took the razor blade and picked the lock open, all within 20 seconds. I put them on a third time and hit up under the desk instead of down and it again released the dead lock and within 20 seconds was free again. I thought "Boy, this is too easy."

Once the inmates and officers were aboard the aircraft, a 4 motor propeller type plane (C56), and securely in place, the plane piloted by the Border Patrol, took off for Steilacoom Airport, Seattle, Washington. Remembering how easy it was for me to open handcuffs, I decided flying is bad enough but with inmates its worse so I periodically checked the locks and chains during the flight to ensure they were locked and stayed that way. Upon arrival at the airport, we were met by officers from the McNeil Island prison and the transfer of inmates was completed. Normally during the transfers a "prison bus" was waiting and the "inmate chains" would be transported to their new home, another Federal prison.   The officers boarded the plane and returned to San Francisco, arriving back at Alcatraz around midnight. It was a very long and stressful day.

The next morning we repeated the same process, except this time we headed to the Federal prison at Leavenworth, Kansas. This was the first stop en-route to the second of two Federal prisons, the other in Atlanta, Georgia. Inmates who were to remain in Leavenworth were transferred to prison officials; inmates who were to go to the prison in Atlanta, Georgia, were temporarily housed in the Leavenworth prison for the night. The next morning, bright and early, we picked up the inmates to be transported to Atlanta along with several inmates from Leavenworth who were being transferred to Atlanta, boarded the plane and proceeded to Atlanta. After arrival in Atlanta we transferred all the inmates to prison officials, and ended another long and stressful journey. We were off duty that evening and free to relax. The next morning we took a commercial jet back to San Francisco.

I don't recall for sure how many "chains" left the island but I was assigned to five of them (listed below).

11-14-62   to McNeil
1-14-63   to McNeil
1-15-63   to Leavenworth and Atlanta
1-26-63   to Leavenworth and Atlanta
3-21-63   last chain ("The ROCK" was closed)

Another memorable event on Alcatraz occurred when Gordon Gronzo, a guard, stepped down from the dock tower for the last time. Permission to step down was granted by Dick Willard, Acting Warden. I saw Gordon coming down the tower steps with the weapons and was thinking "Don't bring those guns down Gordon!" Emotions of prison personnel were very strong and it was hard to accept that all of the convicts were gone.

In April/May 1963, government furniture that was on the island in various staff housing was made available to be purchased. It wasn't the fanciest furniture in the world, but was solid and would serve us well. We decided to purchase various items and the total cost was $112.00. I said to Cathy "Where can you get this much furniture for this amount of money. " We also knew that it would be shipped at no cost to our new assignment in Marion, Illinois.

$1.00 Chair	$7.50 Vanity
$9.00 3 Box Springs	$8.00 Table
$2.50 Chair	$10.00 Stove
$1.00 Magazine Rack	$18.00 Chest of Drawers
$17.50 Refrigerator	$12.50 Davenport
$9.00 2 Beds	$15.00 3 Mattresses
$ 1.00 Bench	

We still have many of these pieces of furniture in our home today.

I was initially scheduled to leave Alcatraz for Marion on April 14, 1963, along with 7 other guards. However, my effective date of transfer was delayed until June 22, 1963. The warden had made arrangements for my family and I to remain on Alcatraz after all the inmates had left because my daughter, Donna, who was born March 10, 1963, had a foot condition for which she was receiving treatment at Kaiser Hospital in San Francisco. Also, I had approved vacation and travel time which set my new date at June 22, 1963, to report to Marion.

From the time the last inmate departed Alcatraz, March 21, 1963, and until my family and I departed the Island in June 1963, my duties were numerous and varied. One of my primary functions included keeping curious people off the island. I patrolled the island with a bullhorn telling people to stay-off the island. Many felt that because it was closed as a prison that it was an open invitation for them to visit. After they discovered that they weren't allowed on the island, they quit trying. Approximately 30 employees, staff and guards remained to keep the island running. We worked 12 hour shifts.

The control center was moved to the visitor's room as a lot of the equipment, i.e., weapons, keys, etc., were being removed and sent to other Federal Prisons. I answered the phone and many questions. The boat radio was also relocated to the visitor's room. With many of the island personnel being transferred to other prisons, I helped loading furniture, equipment, etc., on the barges to leave the island for Fort Mason and ultimately their new locations. It felt very strange seeing the cellhouse empty and not having to keep looking over my shoulder.

During our last few weeks on Alcatraz, my family had the opportunity of a lifetime, to go anywhere and everywhere on the island, including the cellhouse which was off limits before. We visited every area within the prison and the outside facilities and even went up into the various towers. All the remaining families on the island took advantage of this opportunity. It was an experience of a life time that was afforded to only a few individuals. Cathy and Kenny talk about it today. Kenny liked bringing my lunch to me during the evening when I was in the control center. On one occasion when he was coming up the steps behind apartment Building A, he fell, dropping the thermos bottle and breaking it. It really upset him. We took a lot of pictures of my family in different areas of the prison and they bring back many fond and enjoyable memories. Cathy stated "Our children will have many stories to tell their friends and our grandchildren."

One evening after dark, Bill Bones (staff member) and his wife Rosie were making a complete tour of the prison. They walked around the island, through industries, up the stairs to the recreation yard wall, across the yard, up the steps and into the cellhouse through the rear door. Bill went to the inmates visiting window at the east end of the cellhouse (near the main gate), and he sent Rosie to ring the bell to get through the gate. He wanted to see me jump when the bell rang. He was successful. It not only surprised me, but startled me. I knew nobody was in the cell blocks and I didn't anticipate the bell ever ringing again. Bill and Rosie were also transferred to Marion, Illinois.

On June 22, 1963, I made history. I was the LAST GUARD OUT. I locked the gate and still have the key. I boarded the boat for the last time as a guard on Alcatraz. I thought to myself, what an experience I had just completed, and how fast the time went by. I felt tears grow in my eyes as the boat went across the water to Fort Mason. I thought: Here's another interesting trivia question - "Who was the last guard out?" I, of course know the answer "James Albright."

ABOUT THE AUTHOR

I started work at Alcatraz on August 24, 1959 as a young man with no prior law enforcement experience. While working on Alcatraz, I received two promotions due to my over all work ethic and proper responses during stressful situations. This included working the control center during the last two escape attempts. After Alcatraz closed, I spent the next twenty two years at various positions at several other prisons before retiring from Terre Haute, Indiana in 1985. Those twenty two years were filled with various experiences and challenges such as riots, food/work strikes, and escape attempts. I captured three Petersburg, Va. escapees while I worked at that institution. Although my twenty six years of prison service were filled with many memories, Alcatraz will always remain the highlight of my law enforcement career.